Sometimes,
Enough
Is Enough

Also by Marsha Sinetar

Ordinary People as Monks and Mystics
Do What You Love, the Money Will Follow
Elegant Choices, Healing Choices
Living Happily Ever After
Developing a Twenty-first-Century Mind
Reel Power: Spiritual Growth Through Film
A Way Without Words
To Build the Life You Want, Create the Work You Love
The Mentor's Spirit
Why Can't Grown-ups Believe in Angels?
(illustrated children's book)
Spiritual Intelligence

Sometimes, Enough Is Enough

Finding Spiritual Comfort in a Material World

Marsha Sinetar

Cliff Street Books

An Imprint of HarperCollins*Publishers*

Case examples are fictionalized and not meant to represent a specific individual. Neither publisher, proprietor, nor author assumes any liability for the use or misuse of methods described, and nothing in this book is intended as a substitute for competent therapy or professional attention.

SOMETIMES, ENOUGH IS ENOUGH. Copyright © 2000 by Sinetar & Associates, Inc. All rights reserved. Printed in the United States of America. No part of this book may be used or reproduced in any manner whatsoever without written permission except in the case of brief quotations embodied in critical articles and reviews. For information address HarperCollins Publishers Inc., 10 East 53rd Street, New York, NY 10022.

HarperCollins books may be purchased for educational, business, or sales promotional use. For information please write: Special Markets Department, HarperCollins Publishers Inc., 10 East 53rd Street, New York, NY 10022.

FIRST EDITION

Designed by William Ruoto

Printed on acid-free paper

Library of Congress Cataloging-in-Publication Data

Sinetar, Marsha.
    Sometimes, enough is enough : finding spiritual comfort in a material world / Marsha Sinetar. — 1st ed.
        p. cm.
    ISBN 0-06-019632-7
    1. Spiritual life—Christianity. I. Title.
BV4501.2.S47275 2000
248.4—dc21   00-025346

00 01 02 03 04 ❖/HC 10 9 8 7 6 5 4 3 2 1

Dedicated to dear friends
Carol Aaron
Jo Ann Ridley
Sister Florence Vales
Monastery of Saint Clare

Acknowledgments

Writing is solitary work, but the production of a book is collaborative, a true community affair. Many skillful people helped bring this volume into being. My thanks to Elaine Markson and Gary Johnson for patience during an incredibly long preparation period; to Diane Reverand, publisher and editor-in-chief of Cliff Street Books, for editing the early manuscript in ways that greatly refined and clarified the final version; to Janet Dery, whose exceptional attention to detail kept us all on schedule despite a fast-track agenda and my own frequent travels. I am grateful to all of you. However, it was Ray Sinetar who gave me heart to continue when it seemed this book would never see the light of day. I appreciate this more than words can say.

The morbid logician seeks to make everything lucid, and succeeds in making everything mysterious. The mystic allows one thing to be mysterious, and everything else becomes lucid.

—G. K. Chesterton, *Orthodoxy*

Contents

Foreword

Do you remember David, that shining lad who triumphed over a terrifying warrior-hulk? David was the youngest in his family. He was a country boy, a sheepherder of sorts. Goliath was the giant who wore a mighty brass helmet, a coat of heavy mail and carried a spear whose head, all by itself, weighed "six hundred shekels of iron" (1 Samuel 17:7). David directly apprehended the power of God. He felt ready to do battle. He marched off to confront Goliath, consoling his clan and asked, "Who is this enemy that he should defy the entire army of the living God?" As Goliath advanced enraged, in an uproar, and yelling curses, David remained poised. He held his own, thundering back, "You may come at me with sword, spear and material might, but I come to you in the name of the Lord of Hosts."

When I heard that story in childhood, I wanted what David had.

Who does not want David's inner fortitude or yearn to live an effective, overcoming life? Who doesn't secretly long to know what he or she could accomplish in a wide-open universe or yearn to express the courage of deeply held convictions? That's the good life that theologian Paul Tillich said gives evidence of "The powerful soul."[1] Knowing we have the courage to *be* who we are is spiritually comforting for we live most meaningfully when our enjoyments affirm destiny's call.

Spiritual comfort is never about avoiding the hassles that come from meeting the unknown. Our deepest satisfactions arrive as we express ourselves distinctively. Or extricate ourselves from some seemingly impossible complication. Situationally speaking, spiritual comforts differ. Spiritual relief is found at the point of our need when something shifts for the better. However, in each case, unless we possess the mental poise and inner trust to get through the dark night of trouble, we'll run from challenge. Without solid fortitude we hide from our giants or seek rescuers to do battle for us. Without spiritual comfort, we forfeit the shimmering potential of our own "good life."

Of course, experiencing a sublime spiritual comfort like David's depends on doing our part. David's walk in life was hardly passive. David was bold and self-assured. He was virtuous, empowered from within. He could afford to walk his talk and demonstrate an active faith because he knew beyond all doubt that he was safe in the undergirding arms of the divine Love. David had meditated on the word of the Lord throughout his young life. When he heard Goliath's ragings and saw weapons aimed against him, he controlled his negative emotions. Being passionate about God, David was dispassionate about surface appearances. He reflected a superior, triumphant reality *because* his mind was at one with Ultimate Reality.

That's the mental turning I'll examine in these chapters. Spiritual comfort, however framed, depends entirely on that deepest loyalty to self-originating Life, or Love, willing and fully able to surpass itself, through us, *as* us.

A mental turning, or conversion, like David's is relatively straightforward. Saints, mystics, and metaphysicians have been describing it for aeons. It's also unconventional. (In the past, one could be crucified for even aspiring to such spiritual heights.) And another catch: There's work for us to do. In *The Philokalia,* a collection of texts written between the fourth and fifteenth centuries by spiritual masters of the Orthodox Christian tradition,[2] we learn that peace, the deepest spiritual comfort, means deliverance from agitation of every sort. That assurance arrives only by the action of the Holy Spirit. In other words, to gain spiritual comfort we must train our thoughts to become servants of the Good.[3]

Even our most modest daily challenges ask us to display steadiness of intent, reliable composure, presence of mind. If, for example, we fly off the handle each time our coworkers suggest a schedule change, word will get around. We'll sorely limit our own opportunities for professional advancement. If we're slyly counterproductive, people will talk. Our own lack of virtue and manipulations will work against us. When we're on a job interview or negotiating a new family tradition with our in-laws, we'll want discernment, confidence, and enough leadership skill to speak forthrightly. David models that exact poise under pressure. It's a mind-set that never goes out of style. David demonstrated influence and skill. He had the ability to handle bullies because he trusted an unseen Protector. David had the most powerful spiritual support in this or any other era: the God-consciousness that releases overcoming power and gets the job done. That knowing is spiritual comfort.

This is not a "self-improvement" book. It is not about developing charisma or controlling bullies or managing stress. Yet a deeply spiritual mind delivers all such goods. In these pages I'll explore the most basic spiritual transformation, the shift from what is often called our "old," or appearance-driven, mind to a new mind—the spiritual sensibility that saints, mystics, and metaphysicians seek: the Mind of God. The methods I'll describe can shift our entire orientation, over time, toward God's thoughts. These, we read in the book of Isaiah (55:8), are not like our thoughts, being qualitatively superior to our usual mind-chatter. Meditative tasks are involved in gaining the mind we want. We'll need to infuse our awareness with right ideas, God's thoughts. Then, too, a reliable poise under pressure asks us to turn from external motivations to inner leadings. The contemplative route that this book describes can lead us directly there.

The path is timeless. By and large it's inflexible, and the bulk of each chapter explores that route—offers practical strategies to help us decide how to integrate prayer and meditation into our busy lives. You'll find concrete stories about people, many of whom I know, who in their own fashion have aligned their routines to the contemplative way despite hefty responsibilities. Before offering some first definitions about what I call a "casual contemplative" life, a few words more about spiritual comfort are in order.

What's Spiritual Comfort?

Comfort means relief or consolation in affliction, as well as "the what" or "the who" that provides our supportive upliftment. We find worldly comforts, particularly in affluent Western society, everywhere. We eat comfort foods. We feel secure when we have money in the bank. We sleep better when we're well insured, or perhaps living in gated communities, or with people of our own age and ilk.

For enduring relief of stress and agitation we must proceed another way, seeking our consolations from our Creator. That's where a casual contemplative life enters the scene: practiced faithfully, these disciplines and especially the mind-set of the life itself unites us with what's real. Thomas Merton once noted our problems come because we're rooted in unreality. A meditative way of being is not about stress-free living. Rather, it orients us toward a rock-solid trust in God, ultimate Reality.

God, to me, is not hovering over humankind as an ominous, punitive force. When that great mystic Meister

Eckhart acknowledged that God's is-ness "is *my* is-ness, neither less or more, [but] wholly equal, and close beside, not beneath there or above there, but just equal, [emphasis added]"[4] he expressed my sentiments, if not those of most contemplatives.

That knowing is critical to the discussion at hand. Contemplative prayer and meditation stem from the most venerable monastic tradition. They've been handed down through the generations for a reason: they work. These disciplines strengthen intimacy, trusting communion, and union with the Spirit of the living God. That oneness is our life's goal although often we're unaware of it. The goal is universal. The wish to attain what I view as David's level of inner fortitude rests within each soul. No one is excluded from the promise of which I write.

When Mahatma Gandhi said that there are two aspects to life, the outward and the inward, he also conceded that the outward was meaningless for him except insofar as it helped the inward.[5] God, or the spiritual Source (which Gandhi tended to call Truth), provided him with the wherewithal to demonstrate his nonviolent principle amid the violent social and political setting of his era. Like David, Gandhi's words and actions direct us yet again to the contemplative conditions of that valor, that good life.

To feel settled on the inside, we must willingly give our attention and allegiance to "the inner." True comfort begins on the inside. That principle is repeated in each chapter.

Gandhi, like David, repeatedly aligned his spiritual ideals with effective, practical actions. That alignment, expressed in Western terms, may be called "works." For instance, in the Bible when we read that without works our faith is dead—impotent—we're being instructed how to live effectively—with valor and virtue and, yes, even spiritual comfort. The opening lines of Psalm 91 take another look at that, restating the obvious prerequisite: *If we dwell in the secret place of the most High, we shall abide under the shadow of the Almighty.* Note the conditional *if*. Again, a contemplative mentality and the life itself, what with its meditative, spiritual focus fulfills Psalm 91's tall order. *If* we turn toward the infinite, divine Intelligence alive *and as* our own consciousness, *if* we adopt a transcendent prayer life and contemplative simplicity we receive the grace, the sweetness and the Presence of God with us. We gain a wholly new mind. Whatever our spiritual heritage, we can follow the instruction of 2 Chronicles 20:17 to

> set yourselves, stand ye still, and see the salvation of the
> Lord with you . . .
> fear not, nor be dismayed, tomorrow go out against them:
> for the Lord will be with you.

Relief from daily pressure flows from the settled ground of being that a contemplative life cultivates. In truth, spiritual comfort is not precisely a contemplative's goal. It's a by-product of something much more glorious: union with, or direct experience of, the Divine. The good news is that glory, the hidden aspiration of each heart, is at hand.[6]

Introduction: First Words

Every man at the beginning doth set forth good wine;
and when men have well drunk, then that which is
worse: *but* thou hast kept the good wine until now.
—John 2:10

Once upon a time, there lived two children whose secret hearts housed secret dreams. Each longed to become royalty of sorts—a *self*-ruler, not a dominator of others. Each wanted the heroic adventure read about in fairy tales—the full-blown triumph over tests and trials that results in joy, safety, and everlasting peace. True freedom. As they grew up, those children embraced different realities.

One lost his heart to a brutal logic that said spiritual reveries were childish, far-fetched, and impractical. The other clung to childhood's hope. She sensed untold, inebriating beauty in an inner promise. Dreams could come true, she thought, if only one graduated from the world of make-believe to the one of unwavering faith, pluck, and spiritual maturity. Trusting her deep instincts, the second child vowed to actualize her spiritual dreams.

The art of contemplation involves that vow. It can restore dreams and spiritual confidence. The same contemplative practices used by our ancient, desert mothers and fathers can connect us to our wholesome yearnings for spiritual victory. These disciplines also cultivate the power to pursue that wholeness. We've had this goal since childhood. When using the word *dreams* I don't mean escapism, but the images of what-could-be that prod us out of our comfort zones. A holy—whole—ideal keeps us inching toward a healthy autonomy, a high life of productive contribution. This book can help *almost* all of us cultivate a contemplative approach to life wherever we now find ourselves—in a city apartment, a suburban tract house, a thatched cottage by the sea.

Whether we're the parents of two-year-olds or we're Wall Street bankers or short-order cooks at Denny's, when it comes to the fulfillment of spiritual dreams, *state of mind matters more than change of circumstance.* Most books that begin with the "mind over matter" refrain discuss positive thinking, but in this book contemplative thought and its benefits are the keys.

The contemplative mode of being is reflective and attentive. It is a state of mind that considers eternal things without dreaminess. Should you inhabit that lucidity, you're contemplative. You recognize that the Spirit undergirds all things at all times, and your bliss comes from dwelling on that idea and, progressively, living in light.

Put simply, state of mind—not materiality—creates your states of harmony, assurance, and comfort. Put simpl*est,* with but a few adjustments you *can* bloom spiritually, right where you're planted.

I've grubbed around in my bank of experience for some ideas I want to share. I've dug about in memory and in my research files for anecdotes about ordinary people—many neighbors, some friends, some strangers I've met on planes—who are flourishing spiritually. A few go to church. Others are unchurched. A rare handful are cloistered, but the great majority are not. I call the latter "casual contemplatives." They are—*we* are—informally, progressively reflective. We share a way of looking at situations and an active life that is contributive by virtue of a daily renewal of spiritual awareness. Paraphrasing William Blake, that renewal happens as our "Immortal Eyes" gaze deeply inward, into the World of Thought.

Since 1973, my own life has included increasingly contemplative elements: prayer, meditation, the reading and mulling over of Scripture. I love solitude and stillness. Time spent agreeably in nature is precious. I even contemplate as I cook.

Well into adulthood, and much like that second child mentioned earlier, I revived an old dream with childhood roots. That dream is humankind's aggregate musing about transcendence. It is generic and it is global. The secret heart of people everywhere, of all ages and backgrounds, beats with a collective yearning for love, peace, inner affluence—true wealth. Perhaps you've tucked away a spiritual vision of that sort in your own heart. Perhaps you've discounted it as "just a fairy tale." If you wonder how to realize your light of intelligence, read on. It is possible to flourish spiritually in a material world.

The Primacy of Spiritual Dreams

To get started, it helps to remember that the fairy tale is a dramatic projection of the life of our psyche. Its themes are relevant to us as contemporary adults. Scholars point to the links between fairy tales and the primitive myths of humankind. Flights from danger, a trial or two to test our mettle, and hardship develop real-world skills, self-knowledge, and inner strength. Spiritual stories end in supernatural triumph: One's long suffering ends in splendor. Another's death begets eternal life. These plot lines assure us that we can live "happily ever after."[1] Given the primacy of such dreams, we tend to read our favorite fables, folktales, and parables repeatedly and imaginatively—first to ourselves. Then to our children. Then again to our grandchildren. Crowds pay rapt attention (and high ticket prices) when movies—usually from Disney, Spielberg, or Lucas—retell these stories. Why? Because the high-flying tales of childhood, while rooted in youthful fantasy, actually have a concrete developmental *purpose* for human growth. We are born for the interior kingdom. Stories that acknowledge the supernatural tap into an ageless wish to be, do, and actualize heroic desires. They permit and encourage a noble, *spiritual* overcoming—striving, reaching, moving beyond comfortable limits. Fables, fairy tales, and certainly the parables of Scripture encourage the illogical faith that, ultimately, opens our Immortal Eyes.

Simultaneously, such stories teach us how to meet practical difficulties. Our heroes and heroines endure. They plan, even scheme, escape from villains and from suffering. They control themselves and manage their emotions. They succeed. They reflect the elemental, celestial longing of *all* people to be free, authentic—true to self and other—and compassionately liberated, healthfully independent and interdependent. We too dream such dreams. We long to be boldly contributive, unrestricted, simultaneously blessed *and* a blessing. That wish is both spiritually and humanly sound.

Moreover, we diverse earthlings share at least one challenge: our spiritual dreams ask us to *choose,* to lean on faith, to develop virtue—power—and a productive, healthy imagination as we tackle our unknowns. Digging within for a workable faith and probing our depths for creative ideas are two aspects of contemplation. Sometimes we need answers—and fast. Something risky or uncharted summons us. Try as we might to figure out a logical approach to our sacred aspirations, sometimes we're stumped. We need to sort through the best ideas. To see truly we must travel to that infinite storehouse of viable answers within. Here's when pluck and competence and trust count most. It's the "fool on the hill," the one with imagination and rock-solid, one-pointed faith, who slays dragons and demons and Goliaths victoriously. *That's* a spiritual triumph, and it's awe-inspiringly practical.

This notion is only loosely wrapped. Gray areas and paradoxes jut out all over the place. If you're seeking thirty-day guarantees or need a crisply linear, military approach to the topic, look elsewhere. You won't find warranties here. The issues of our human heart may be poetic and eternal, but frankly, they're untidy. As a friend says, "Life is messy and *we're* messy, and we just have to press forth in love in spite of it all."

Contemplative life and its disciplines incorporate so much more than slaying dragons. For we are human and unique, and to be a particular human being "is only possible because of [God's] Presence," and as the French monk Abhishiktānanda, who lived in India, also wrote: "There is no part of our life in which we can escape the mystery of God . . . to lead a contemplative life is nothing else than to live in the actual presence of God."[2]

Nonetheless, what I have to say is practical, especially for artists, poets, entrepreneurial or inventive sorts, and spiritual daydreamers. Quite a lot of us, as it turns out. As reviewed in chapter 1, millions—maybe billions—of us cling to our "illogical" musings. Universally speaking, our spiritual dreams are alive and kicking. We crave the spiritual comfort of inner peace. We seek overarching meaning in our work and relationships. We want our children to inherit sturdy spiritual values. We wish them enduring joy and harmony. We want to execute our lifetime purposes with style and precision, and we yearn to live in safe, cooperative, compassionate communities. These are spiritual comforts.

We hear a growing cry from the corporate sector about the desirability of merging spirit and work. Every week some magazine or news report extols "new" benefits to be derived from achieving balance in life. We're admonished to simplify and scale back excessive activities and grow more productive, stress-free, healthier. Let's face it, that's old news. The saints and mystics have always preached simplification. Let's get on with the *living* of such edicts. Let's walk our spiritual talk.

In that vein, I'll share some concrete tools to help you merge your "spirit and work." *Nearly* anyone can adjust a hectic, out-of-control schedule and gain more of what's truly worthwhile *if* priorities are set and certain critical fundamentals are found and followed. I'll offer some practical keys that, at least for me, have been fundamental to unlocking a deep spiritual renewal. For example, we can:

- Manage time (especially the way we start and end each day)
- Limit exploitive encroachments in favor of developing a clear spiritual focus
- Learn what it means for us *as individuals* to pray "in the Spirit"

As you read, please keep one point in mind: your productivity and worldly success are not my main focus now. It's your secret heart, your finest, healthiest spiritual dream, and your sane, positive determination that I'd like to restore and bolster. I want to return you to your true self. Apparently that's what I do. I'm good at it, and I've done it for *years*—for myself as well as for students, clients, and readers whose ages have ranged from five to ninety-something. For that encouragement, nothing beats contemplative prayer and a casually reflective life. It lifts us up. Calms us down. Centers us. Unleashes confidence and imaginative flair. Contemplative disciplines *may* lead to social action. Or they may not. That's a separate issue. How socially active you are, and how meditative, depend on your disposition, your talent, your life's purpose—your calling. Both social action and contemplation depend on vocation, a topic I've written about extensively and will only touch on here.[3]

Over time even an informal contemplative discipline produces inner benefits, particularly trust in God—a word I define, in part, as unoriginated, immutable, eternal life, and as self-sustained creative power and absolute holiness.[4] My focus is on establishing an intimate, right relationship with God and in the context of a contemplative adventure I define *casual* as

- unceremonious, but not sloppy;
- relaxed and trusting, but not random;
- spontaneously intuitive, but not wildly irregular; and
- *moderately* disciplined but not rigid, inflexible, or hurtfully ascetic.

I do not interpret the word *casual* to mean tepid or hit-or-miss. May it never be said that a contemplative is blasé. In this connection, to be lukewarm is counterproductive.

Father Borst pinpoints exactly *how* to become a contemplative. He frames much, but not all, of what I plan to say:

> *There is only one way to become a contemplative and that is by setting aside each day, or regularly, some time and place for prayer that is real, personal and contemplative. Without the practice of contemplative prayer, no individual and no community can be called contemplative. No amount of other prayers and occupations can make up for this need. If, then, you wish to become a contemplative, get down to making yourself available for contemplative prayer every day.*[5]

Overview

In chapter 1, I'll talk about getting started and explore some reasons why contemplative practices (what I generally refer to as "praying in the Spirit," or what we could call transcendent, self-forgetful prayer) seem, to me, more advanced and *vastly superior* to popular goal-setting and affirming techniques. Chapter 2 expands that discussion, and in chapter 3 I show how each individual's spirituality and interior directives are "one of a kind." A divine DNA makes us who we are, while linking us appropriately to others. To find your right *form* of contemplative prayer, find your unique spiritual fingerprint. If you find and honor that, bliss is assured.

Later chapters explain why contemplative practices

*un*complicate us and also propose that contemplative prayer is not precisely a procedure. It is a state of being, a stance of mind, a posture of the heart that flows from faith in the Spirit infusing all life. That state may have been what Gandhi meant by "heart culture." It is a way of being fully present while attending to grubby routines or relating forthrightly or patiently to others—a principle of faith, experience itself.

Each chapter contains an application exercise. This is for consideration, and not offered as a "Thou Shalt." In such matters, wisdom evaluates a practice before going hog-wild with it and never forces anything. Chapter 7's summary includes several meditations designed to help the interested envision how to put all this into action, in privacy, and in laid-back fashion. At least to start with.

Which brings up one secret of contemplative life. If we're truly called to it—and I mean roused to contemplation according to God's "purpose and grace" (2 Timothy 1:9)—then the more pure stillness we experience, the more we'll want. Practiced rightly, contemplation offers us the drink of "good wine" that has been kept until now. Who can resist? It is divinely intoxicating.

1

Shouldering the Beams of Love

Return to thy rest, O my soul;
For the Lord hath dealt bountifully with thee.

—Psalms 116:7

It is said that the friends of an old desert monk pleaded with him to discontinue his asceticism. He stuck to his ways, replying, "I tell you my children that Abraham, when he saw the great gifts of God, had to repent for not having striven beforehand."[1]

So it goes with those of us who seek a simple, reflective life. Our companions may grumble. They warn us away from our changes. They fret. They cling. They give advice and caution reasonably, "It's foolhardy to try to shape a contemplative's lifestyle without joining a cloistered community. Don't buck convention."

So it went with me. As I made plans to live a casual, secular, contemplative life, my worldly colleagues got out of joint. Edgy. The traditionally minded—those who have been called the active livers and householders—counseled against a solitary life. They called it "treacherous" and warned me, "Be careful. Don't move out to the hinterlands on your own." When I drove off in my little blue Honda for the lush, green hills of northern California, most scoffed, "How will you earn a living? Who will you turn to in that remote spot if things sour? Hardier types than you have failed."

I'd considered that. I knew myself. I knew then (and more so now) that my naysayers were simply being overcautious. My mind's eye could *see* the life I wanted. Crystal clear. I was not seeking an easy life but rather the tenacity to meet the demands that flow out of answering an authentic call. I wanted challenge—a holy adventure. Plus, I needed something new by which to understand everything old. Like it or not, I had entered G. K. Chesterton's world of "elfland" where, *if* we are sane, a kind of worldly reasonableness makes us nutty. An Amanda Cross character—Harriet, the "imperfect spy"—captures another elusive element of my intended revolt. As Harriet explains, healthy revolt begins when we question societal "shoulds":

Always beware of people with principles. I don't mean general principles like the Golden Rule, or that Hebrew who stood on one foot and said something about treating one's neighbor as oneself. I mean people who grab onto a structure, usually one that's been in place, untested, for years, maybe for centuries, and feel so cozy inside it that they don't want to be moved out.[2]

I'd squandered too many years living under a cloud of dread, dutifully, secretly outer-directed. And I felt anxious. The subtlest expectation of my elders became my command. That had to stop. It was time to break out of that rut. Sometimes, enough *is* enough.

Today, some twenty years after leaving a cozy conventional nest for my wilderness of choice, I feel like Abraham gazing upon God's great gifts: I repent for not beginning this adventure sooner, and wonder why I've stalled my next steps, which puzzle, nudge, and beckon even as I write.

Pure stillness draws me ever deeper into stillness—into the more profound silence of foreign, uncharted woods and an easygoing, reflective life, the structures and self-disciplines that gather no moss. One is not always thinking, *I* should *do this now . . .* , or, *I shouldn't* do that. . . . What a gigantic relief. Given a proper focus for each day, the tasks and movement of the day are just appropriate to its purposes.

On some tape or other, when he was asked how to tell if one were spiritually illumined, Thomas Merton cited an ancient Buddhist precept: "When you're hungry you eat. When you're tired you sleep." Precisely. *That's* casual. While that's a soothing thought, such fuzzy rules of thumb are what most of us cannot stand, no less fulfill, mired as we are in overeating (or dieting) and in oversleeping (or insomnia), obsessed as we are with doing what we *think* is expected. We need a healthy imagination to break out of ruts. We need wholesome autonomy, the ability to say, "Yes," "No," and, "No more of that for me, thanks," as if we mean it. We need a holy ideal to aim at "or what's a Heaven for?" All the propriety and reasonableness in the cosmos cannot deliver the benefits of a vision of spiritual possibilities.

For that well-honed vision, contemplation is a must. We'll want to keep it at the forefront of our mind. Our home is Heaven said the saintly parish-priest John Vianney: "On earth we are like travelers staying at a hotel. When one is away, one is always thinking about going home."[3]

Life in Our "Cell" of Consciousness

As I see it, to be a casual contemplative is to trust what Merton calls "the cell"—the space, time, and conditions of our humdrum life. We'll trust the ordinary roll-out of each day to teach us what we need to know about "going home." In the cell, we'll feel homesick for our sacred truths, and that's a blessing. Homesickness turns us toward the light. It is a truism that to overcome earthly constraints, we must first transcend them from within, correct ourselves on the inside in order to change the outside. Contemplatives sit in their cell to change, or to fly home to Heaven.

One of the first things one learns is that, in a sense, one is completely flawed, not a monk or a contemplative at all, merely a child of Life in the earliest throes of actualizing "the fruitful lessons of solitude."[4] To embrace ironies like that we can't be *too* reasonable. We can't keep polarizing events into "good" or "bad" boxes, and must not be so highbrowed as to reject the lowliest of grungy tasks as holy teachers. Oswald Chambers maintained that, seen rightly, even our shallow, so-called profane concerns are profound. Our ebb and flow of waking up in the morning, drinking coffee, washing the breakfast dishes, and showering is just as much a part of the Divine as anything else: "It is not your devotion to God that makes you refuse to be shallow, but your wish to impress other people with the fact that you are not shallow, which is a sure sign that you are a spiritual prig."[5]

Many of us—the inflexible mostly—cannot absorb such contemplative ideas. Or we misguidedly suppose that because we are blemished—restless, covetous, slothful— we aren't cut out for holiness. Tsk-tsk. This is *self*-hood-winkery—exactly what self-doubt, negativity, and cowardice would have us believe.

No special garb, icons, or credentials are needed to reflect the love of God. The French monk Abhishikt-ānanda, whose Christian spirituality was vivified by living in India, tells us:

> *Truly there is nothing in the created universe, in all time and space, which does not manifest God and reveal his glory to mankind. In creating us God bestowed on us intelligence and reason, thus making us able to recognize his manifestation in the world and in events, so that we might respond to it in love.*[6]

Decades ago it seemed obvious: by taking a few can-
tankerous steps, no more than three or four (like selling
my dust-gathering goods and my tiny vintage home and
plundering my pension plan to finance a relocation), I
could appropriate a life of sacred casualness. I *knew* I
was flawed. Uncertain. Afraid. Still, my mind was made
up. I planned to adopt much the same patterns of behav-
ior as were exemplified by the disciples of Jesus of
Nazareth, namely:

- A rightly ordered life
- An incremental "self-vanishing": the personal ego
  dissolves into or gives way to the Transcendent
- A reoriented loyalty to the inspirations of grace, or
  the Presence of God

I promise you, I didn't know exactly what I was doing.
Had you asked me why, I absolutely could not have
explained. Had you asked me how, I'd have been tongue-
tied. If you'd handed me a blueprint showing me exactly
how to build the life I wanted, I would have gone unconscious—I wouldn't have known what to do with it. (I've
never properly followed a set of written instructions in my
life. To be sure, I have my perfectionistic moments, but
formula-making is not part of that. Not on my screen at
all.) All along I've just clung to the audacious idea that by
leaning on my own peculiar vision of what could be, and
by trusting Scripture and prayer as my primary spiritual
guides, I could shape everyday life to accommodate every
holy desire. So far, so good.

Who Wants Spiritual Comfort?

These days it strikes me that anyone with a little moxie and basic common sense can improvise a way to live, work, and relate that enriches spiritually. With firm intent, it's not *that* tough to arrange an unfettered, worshipful life. Moreover, I wonder why more people don't simply up and do it. It's no secret that *millions* long for a well-lived reality of supernatural love.

More than 51 percent of all Americans value their free time above their money. Nearly half of those polled rank a high-quality spiritual existence right up there in their *top three lifetime priorities*.[7] Eight out of ten Americans would like to grow spiritually (a 24 percent jump in the last four years). There is a national hunger for spiritual comfort, and a growing desire to extinguish the violent streak in our national psyche that, of late, has produced so many school killings. We must remember that even the betterment of society starts with ourselves.

According to an article in the *Christian Science Monitor*, a Gallup poll of 1,200 adults found that Americans want "to reassert the spiritual element" in both their living and their dying. "They want spiritual comfort in the form of prayer and a feeling of closeness *to God*."[8] Millions more must yearn for greater stores of whatever they deem sacred. True, not everyone feels disposed or self-reliant or trusting enough to move to the woods. Nothing says they have to. Fewer still feel called to live alone—separated from the herd. No one says they must. Solitude is not for everyone. Yet surely everyone, and especially children, can benefit from a calm and rightly ordered life.

The properly ordered life is based on a well-kept secret. When we're rightly disposed—what pop culturists term living "balanced" lives—we're a bit disordered, not totally predictable, not always riding on the same wavelength with others. To reach the shores of spiritual maturity, we often swim through turbulent waters. It's well worth the trouble. Spiritual maturity—and its inherent comforts—creates a rightness within. We've gained what Proverbs calls the fountain of life, the joy that's meaningful. Maybe that's why we avoid "balance." Real joy is tough to tolerate. It blows the mind.

Parameters and Background

A separated life need not be bleak or isolated. Creative contributors like painter Georgia O'Keeffe and naturalist-author John Muir were reclusive, but their impressive legacy of works proves that solitaries can be loving and connected, beautifully productive. To be isolated is to be cut off, especially from love. When we feel summoned to live in fruitful solitude, we'll be growing in strength and healthy self-discipline so that we might bear what Douglas Steere insightfully called "beams of love." Steere likened those beams to fire: most of us can't stand the heat. We "fashion protective clothing . . . that resist all radiation, even beam-proof shelters within corporate religious exercises in order to elude 'beams of love' and to stay as [we] are."[9]

To be healthfully solitary is to be tenderly, not brutally, disciplined for the greater good, that we may share our beams of love and best ideas—whatever holiness we directly experience—and inner peace with others (Hebrews 12:10–15). Spiritual comfort flows from that gentle pursuit of self-discipline. Even here we find *degrees*.

Contemplatives tend to converse less and reflect more than most. The "active livers," when they are of a religious temperament, may invent cute little self-improvement programs. They study according to some fixed course or schedule. They pray in obvious ways, usually when there are lots of people around. Contemplatives pray unceasingly, but read sparingly. They wander around a lot. They gaze up at the night sky. They gawk at winking stars and wonder about infinity. They hear their own gladness in bird chirps and children's laughter. They're in the world, yet not precisely of it. It's their life's mission to discover how to love big, yet impersonally and without clutching, as in the beginning. They're the sort to ponder Large Questions while driving over to Sears to buy a wrench:

Who am I really?
Why was I born?
What's my life's purpose?
Have I ever really loved?
What will happen to me after death?

To some extent, all contemplatives—even those with secular involvements—possess the mystic sense that mulls over questions like these. That sense also fuels the love impulse and the awareness behind a singular aim: oneness with the Divine.

What Does the "Mystic Sense" Involve?

Framed in familiar religious terms, the phrase "mystic sense" means we have received the Spirit of God and we perceive and accept all things as freely given from above. Does all this sound vaguely familiar? It should. Humankind has been hearing, reading, and sharing stories with mystical themes for centuries. Be advised: given the era of my experience, my message takes a twenty-first-century turn, but Truth is timeless. Even though little has changed, we mortals seem to require an endless stream of anecdotes about what's real.

My days are ordinary, with one caveat: since 1980 I've inched toward a somewhat solitary, devotional life. It's reflective. Meandering. A tad *too* lighthearted, some might say. Despite a sometimes busy corporate schedule, I'm influenced by monastic—not industrialist—archetypes. Mega-moguls and TV or celebrity tycoons leave me yawning. It's writers like Evelyn Underhill and monks like Thomas Merton who have impressed me. Nor am I emulating that dark, historically grim asceticism according to which ancient self-mortifiers, riddled with guilt, draped black cloth over their windows to prove their worthiness or beat themselves bloody to purify themselves. Far from it. Each day is light-filled. Playful.

Translucent. Mostly I just feel grateful. Like any garden-variety monk.

Who's a Monk?

The monk is a socially transcendent individual who responds to an inner call to *re*interpret his (or her) fundamental way of being in the scheme of things.[10] Work, marriage, friendships, self-definition, family ties—the monk reevaluates all these facets of daily life in the fresh , clean air of spiritual authenticity. In 1985 I wrote that the word *monk* means much more to me than common usage would indicate:

> *I use the term* monk *without reference to gender, marital status, occupation or place of residence, and with full knowledge that people I'd call monks would not, and do not, in fact call themselves monks.*
>
> *[I've] simply needed a term which would embrace the one who, due to an inner prompting, turns from familiar, secure patterns of social customs . . . toward something altogether unknown . . . [I] needed a word that embraced the imagery of silence, dignity and obedience which accompanies [us] when [we] embark upon an interior journey.[11]*

No matter that monks are typically considered men, I relate to the monastic life, the single-minded devotion of it,

and "the flowering of a deeper identity on an entirely different plane from a mere psychological discovery, a paradoxical
new identity that is found only in right relationship and loss
of self."[12] A story about the life of present-day Trappist
monks at the oldest Trappist monastery in America—the
Abbey of Gethsemani in Kentucky—explores this paradox:
When John, a young and frequent visitor to the abbey,
quizzed the well-seasoned Brother Ambrose about what it
means to be a monk, Brother Ambrose explained that monks
are called to live in solitude. Whereupon John replied, "'You
are not alone because you live with God.' After that,
Ambrose took real interest in John."[13] Whatever their gender
or doctrinal mind-set, genuine monks live in intimate relationship with God. That alone prevents priggishness. Also
monks learn not to direct their goals too rigidly. They pray
unceasingly in order to stay open, to take things as they
come—both the obviously good and the camouflaged.

Worldly Versus Meditative "Goals"

The conventionally minded, when newly aware of their
inner depths, realize that their subjective world can be a
powerful creative ally. Naturally, they begin to experiment
with goal setting techniques. In fact, what we normally
think of as "goal setting" encompasses many practical
spiritual techniques: keeping a journal, using positive
affirmations, practicing visualization. Such methods can
enhance our ability to heal when we're ill. They can
improve our financial affairs, and sustain a prosperity-

consciousness once we have it. Many meditative practices—for instance, relaxation, breathing and certain yoga techniques—are productive stress management devices. These spiritual practices have been hijacked by glitzy self-improvement entrepreneurs and the industrial world. When people seek worldly power instead of pure awareness, they'll try anything. In this case, entry into meditation seems productive. However, worldly goals involve "getting." Meditation empties us.

Today colleges, corporations, and retreat centers around the globe (as well as the most blatantly commercial prosperity-seminars) routinely offer a variety of goal-setting activities to people who want to:

- identify and articulate their goals clearly,
- produce time lines for completing these,
- visualize far-off goals as successfully attained,
- create, verbalize, and/or write positive affirmations related to their ambitions.

These largely acquisitive practices have their place, particularly in our schemes of enterprise and achievement. However, overly explicit methods are not exactly monk-like and generally these constitute only the grossest introduction to meditation. The first skates over surface waters; the latter—true meditation—deep-sea dives for the Pearl of Great Price. There is a vast divide between the world of elementary goal-setting and the cosmos of stillness, prayer, and meditation.

True meditation invites the subtlest of subtle experiences, concerned as it is with cultivating what author and philosopher Max Picard called the Divine Stillness that *is* a presence. In pure stillness alone we realize that material things appear from the things we cannot see. Claudio Naranjo and Robert Ornstein expertly underscore meditation's *mode of being,* which seeks unity, or merger, with Absolute Reality. However that deeper mode of being shines through experience, it transforms everything for the better:

> *If its medium is movement, it will turn into dance; if stillness, into living sculpture; if thinking, into the higher reaches of intuition; if sensing, into a merging with the miracle of being; if feeling, into love; if singing, into sacred utterance; if speaking, into prayer or poetry; if doing the things of ordinary life, into ritual in the name of God or a celebration of existence.*[14]

In the introduction I defined contemplative prayer as "praying in the Spirit." That act reveals the finest nuances of consciousness. The chief object of that prayer is not simply to be *less* acquisitive but to actually *invert* the grasping, clinging reflex of the world for an inner emptying, detachment from all created things. In every spiritual heritage contemplative prayer draws us to the holy place, the still foundation of things, and the root of our unseen, essential self.

For instance, the aim of most yogic methods is to concentrate the mind on a single point. That process, executed properly, ultimately produces cessation of thought. We are told that "the mental emptiness which is the object of yoga is not, however, sought for its own sake," but to open and awaken us to eternal things.[15] This is what I mean by inner emptying.

Rather than throw out goal-setting methods as so much "baby with the bath water," progress in the contemplative arts encompasses these ideas while also teaching us about single-minded intent and its paradoxical partner, letting go. These two attitudes begin to build our spiritual house on the bedrock of true Source—the activity of God with us and all creation.

Here is a concrete illustration of the letting-go principle: A good friend offered to purchase a seaside lot on which to build her dream house. She was soon tormented by early feedback from the sellers that the deal might sour. Knowing of my interest in spirituality, she asked for a calming thought. I mentioned to her that my outcomes are generally best whenever I've *released* my goals in prayer. The sooner I stop trying to squeeze a guaranteed and specific result out of some ambition, the sooner it, *or something better*, comes to pass. Hearing that last phrase, my friend cheered up considerably. She explained, "Oh, you're describing the Law of Nonresistance." Then she elaborated: A harmonious consciousness begets success. Like a game of tug-of-war, as soon as you let go of your rope of self-will, you win. She added that she would immediately begin cultivating a nonresistant mind.

For the next two days my friend strolled around her prospective land while meditating on one idea: *This or something better*. At night, when sleep eluded her because she was worrying about the escrow, she repeated the thought: *This property or something better.* The next week she reported that the sellers had agreed to her terms. Her escrow was back on a solid track.

Subsequently, at a used bookstore, I found these words in a slim pamphlet with old yellowed pages:

[Nonresistance is] a positive approach which offers no opposition, and does not take opposition into account.

If you are nonresistant toward years, the passing of the years will not age you. You continue, but you do not grow old. Your life is transferred from time to eternity. States of consciousness come and are succeeded by other states, but you do not die; you continue to live.

When you are nonresistant toward your good, your good runs to meet you. I have found that I never win until I become willing to do without the trophy.[16]

To restate the obvious: contemplative practices are *nonac-*quisitive. How then does letting go of anxious effort become a key to worldly success? By relinquishing our emotional fixation on a particular outcome, by sitting in silence before God, we release the Holy Spirit to act freely for this or for something *much* better. And in the Spirit's timing: "It is indeed so difficult for us not to be constantly either rushing ahead of or lagging behind the Spirit; we are always so eager to know and act on our own and at our own speed."[17]

Letting go of anxious efforts to control events is an

important ingredient of fulfilling achievement. To prosper spiritually, *before* setting goals, we quiet down. We listen inwardly. Instead of getting frantic about some project gone awry, we clear the deck of our awareness of distracting, surface aims. With deeper awareness guiding us, prior to initiating business or personal objectives, we will *hear* our interior directives. In part, that's what it means to become "meek" in spirit—desiring nothing, becoming self-less. Relinquishment of willful plotting in prayer allows a high spiritual intelligence to influence our life. In simple still-ness, we return to the Source of all good, that our life with the world of things might be infused with the aims and attributes of the Spirit.[18]

Contemplative prayer, if it aims at anything, seeks God's peace. If we're monklike, then we sit receptively before God in stillness, open to the radical insight—quite possibly an illogical knowing—of what wants to happen through our life, through our words and deeds. That's the discipline and silent Presence that organizes contemplative life. Our disci-pline of awe helps us shoulder "beams of love."

IDEAS FOR THE SPIRITUAL WALK

Find Time for Contemplative Prayer

Step 1: Establish a Contemplative Habit

For the next week or so, consider making it your top pri-ority to establish a time and place where you will be undis-turbed for somewhere between five and thirty minutes.

Your extended objective is first to make a habit of some prayer-practice and then to integrate a contemplative pattern into your regular life. A bedroom, a den, an enclosed patio, your home-office, even a bathroom—any of these spaces could provide periods of solitude. Use your imagination. Locate a safe, private nook that is predictably secluded. Examine the contemplative practices of your own, or a favored, spiritual tradition.

Experiment. Try out one spot for a day or two. Try another for a second spell. After locating a private place and a quiet time in the day, explore the possibilities. Sit in simple stillness. Don't monkey with, or try to regulate, your breathing. Just observe it. Let your mind quiet down. Don't force anything. Let your breath become even and "soft." Relax easily into a settled state for three to five minutes. You *can* control your chattering mind—by *not* controlling anything. Just observe your thoughts. That's a meditation. Remember:

> *There is only one way to become a contemplative and that is to set aside each day, or regularly, some time and place for prayer that is real, personal and contemplative.*[19]

Simple sitting may evolve into prayer. It may not. At the very least you might celebrate the moment. That means *enjoy* it. Become attentive to your sitting task. Sit in receptive stillness to whatever's happening. That's a first step to gaining reverential awe.

From what's been said thus far, you'll see that it's possible, in fact it's *necessary*, to adjust your spiritual routines to your ordinary life. It takes intention and sincere, progressive enjoyment of contemplative nondoing. There's no need to run off to an ashram or sit on top of Mount Shasta in stony silence. On the other hand, you never know.

Step 2: Set Up Contemplative Routines in Your Daily Life

After you've designed a time and place for simple, quiet sitting, choose and arrange a basic program of contemplative routines from options such as:

Morning (five to sixty minutes)
Set aside an early morning time of prayer, meditation, and/or reading of a favored scriptural text. Ingesting two or three lines of Scripture along with your morning coffee before the kids are awake will do nicely.

Evening (before sleep)
Pray, meditate, and/or read your favorite sacred text. Or listen to inspirational, spoken word tapes. At night your goal could be to fall asleep with an idea or word of something holy in mind.

Anytime It's Convenient
Pursue one regular physical discipline, such as yoga, t'ai chi, Pilates method, walking, and do so

- routinely
- noncompetitively

- nonaggressively
- concentratedly
- silently (not conversationally)
- at least three times a week for
- at least twenty minutes.[20]

Of course, you'll obtain your doctor's approval and advice before starting anything new of this sort.* And, if you believe you're too busy for daily prayer, you're right. You *are* too busy.

*Seemingly innocuous disciplines like yoga and meditation, especially those that teach us to tinker with our posture and breathing, are powerful transforming agents and must not be taken lightly. People on hypertensive medications or tranquilizers are irresponsible if they begin any meditation routines without first consulting a knowledgeable health care professional for an opinion on such practices.

2

The Hearing Ear, the Seeing Eye

The joy of the Lord is your strength.
—Nehemiah 8:10

Since it's my way to plan things on my own, I prepared for a contemplative life alone. I read several books each month and, concurrently, fragments from countless others.* I mulled over what I read, chewed over everything, kept a motley, dated journal of treasured quotes, and scribbled notes in the margins of my calendar. Stored at the forefront of my mind were spiritual nuggets of pure gold. A few gave me courage to relocate to the redwoods and an informal, reflective life. For example:

1975   The joy of the Lord is your strength.
              (Nehemiah 8:10)

*Some of my favorite books are listed in "Further Reading."

1977	Offer the sacrifices of righteousness, and put your trust in the Lord. (Psalms 4:5)
1980	Believe what is in line with your needs, for only in such a belief is the need fulfilled. (William James)
1980	When someone told Emerson that the world was going to end the next day, he said, "That's all right with me. I can get along without it; I've gotten along without it for a long time." (Quoted from a book by Ernest Holmes)

That naturalist-monk (and, to me, casual contemplative) John Muir considered Nature his good mother who "sees well to the clothing of her many bairns."[1] Saint Francis viewed Nature as his sister, and "even a younger sister: a little, dancing sister."[2] Either way, mother or sister, father or friend, it's clear that Nature is good medicine for a contemplative's heart, as Saint Bernard of Clairvaux wrote in his 106th Epistle: "We'll find something more in woods than in our books. Trees and stones teach us what we can never learn from masters."[3]

Thus it comes to pass that now each dawn I rise to greet the unspoiled day in wonder. Living near a rural expanse as I do, I see miracles in the prosaic: in yellow buds and chartreuse tree frogs the size of your pinkie and in shards of sunlight streaming through the pines. Keep in mind I am a lowbrow. As such, I impress easily. But I regress.

I was only going to say that by moving to the country, life improved. By integrating my spiritual realities with what some call the profane, I now have oodles of time to spend industriously, and a bit of it for socializing, and the bulk of it to use alone. Without interruption. Meditatively. And that's what I love most. Nor am I the only one.

Spiritual Listening as Disposition, Not Technique

In their letter exchanges, two modern contemplatives and long-distance friends explain why a meditative life is crucial for their well-being. One, a cloistered nun, writes of her order's "Martha and Mary" retreats wherein the participants receive great value from taking turns at contemplation:

> *The Marthas are in retreat but do the necessary chores, and the Marys need not do any. Then the next time the roles change. It works out beautifully. We used to pay a priest to preach to us; now we just have what we call a private retreat with Father P.W. giving us a good homily at the Mass. Sisters read their own topics, listen to tapes, and just enjoy.*[4]

Reading those lines, one can picture ways that modern family life could be revived—stress lowered, intimacy strengthened, children soothed, spiritual growth enhanced—if parents adopted those sorts of cooperative solutions. Mary's inner stance is worshipfully committed. Her mode of being, her disposition, and not her self-help tricks, lets her attend to what Life has to say. Spiritual listening is

Mary's vocation, her *top* priority. She's not forcing herself. Interior listening comes first—before an aerobics class, before washing the pesky dishes, before answering her sibling's e-mail. Before *all* else.

Mary's contemplative posture seems spontaneously casual in the way I mean it here. To hold a conversation with her, Jesus didn't need to schedule an appointment. When he dropped in, she dropped whatever she was doing to heed the sayings of her Lord. As we shall see, we can cultivate that disposition. A warning is only fair: if you're summoned to contemplation, the more of it you taste, the more you'll crave. That paying of attention to the inmost Spirit on a second-by-second basis seasons everything for the good.

A contemplative life embodies a spiritual interiority. It is "more like the absorption of a child in play [who is] alert and full of wonder, fascination and love."[5] That life of awe is uniquely suited to those who develop a contemplative *mind*. We're told that means an emptying of "self," what elsewhere I've called self-forgetfulness or self-vanishing. It is, we learn from one anonymous contemplative, "that complete giving-up and giving over of oneself to the Transcendent that Jesus of Nazareth advised when admonishing Martha to correct her priorities. Martha made herself useful, but Mary chose right relationship with Christ."[6]

Incrementally, a relaxed but worshipful reflection transfigures us. It shifts our mind, our heart, our life itself toward the inner union. In no way is that a perfectionistic, legalistic, or nitpicking mentality.

Even the most ascetic contemplative must eventually abandon a fussy, Martha-like striving in favor of that healing relationship with God that honors the best part of the self, which shall never be removed (Luke 10: 38–42). Let us remember that Martha and Mary are part of us. The conflict, as Merton so ably noted, is always within, and must be reconciled within ourselves.

That "best part" may puzzle reasonable worker bees. Ever buzzing, ever bent on doing more, having more, or somehow impressing others with their achievements, the compulsive worker can't possibly be casual at *any*thing. In striving to do *all* things flawlessly, compulsives deprive themselves of a spiritual comfort: the knack, now and then, of taking life as it comes, of simply rejoicing in the moment.

With compassionate self-awareness, contemplatives learn to exercise an existential discretion. To reach the "best part" of themselves, they row their boat of doings with less frenzy. They relinquish worldly enchantments, if only gradually, and that means giving up long-cherished illusions. It's not only what we do, or the quantity of it, that frazzles us, but the motive and interior tone we adopt.

As we discard old, tarnished compulsions, we pay more attention to something new—a heightened appreciation for, say, children, an herb garden, the welfare of a neighbor, or a hobby like quilting, hiking, or bird watching. These are the elemental, existential choices that so helpfully undo the false structures of our life by somehow honoring the true, core self.

To achieve a life of balance, we'll own up to the level of contemplation that's right for us. That involves relaxing our grip on a certain idealizing. We can stop attending obligatory but mind-numbing social functions, or lighten up on our obsessive floor polishing, or reject some fashion nicety to make time for deeper satisfactions.

A former legal secretary (now an entrepreneur) recalls her wasted hours. She spent the better part of every work-day morning attempting to maintain a pleasing corporate image. After attending a few spiritual retreats, she insti-tuted a few changes—mostly to protect her time. She no longer wears tight suits, little bow ties, and binding panty-hose. She says, "You can't imagine the hours and the money that saves." She's still neat and tidy, still a top-notch secretary. She's just put her priorities in proper order for *her* life.

No one can *force* such changes on anyone. We rarely can force them on ourselves. A wholehearted spiritual direction soon alters loyalty, a point that brings up a crit-ical ingredient of contemplative life: gentleness. Coercion is seldom part of the program. Much spiritual turning is gradual. Experimental. *If* we incline ourselves to the beams of light emanating from our depths, our heart hears, or feels, the joy of the Lord. We grow in trust—*emotional* safety. In time we respect the primal dignity of who we are and, spontaneously, begin to select that "best part" of ourselves and of the day that truly fulfills.

The best part of ourselves reveals itself in our finger-print of worship too. Before exploring how spiritualities differ, I must say a word about the psychological compo-nent of wholesome independence. Without that, spiritual progress is fleeting.

Spiritual "Success" Involves Wholesome Autonomy

Wholesome autonomy is *healthy* freedom. That's not license to do anything while trampling on the rights of others; it's a disciplined liberty. Psychologically, wholesome autonomy includes both sensible *in*dependence and *inter*dependence. We are our own. *And* we serve others from the profundities of our distinctive way of being and perceiving the world around us. There's a give-and-take to this, a dovetailing or reciprocity of respect and advantage. If we're *wholesomely* interdependent, we're neither infantile nor so hungry for the approval of others that we're bouncing marionettes, reacting to the whims of whoever pulls our strings. We're helpful, not from neediness, but out of genuine concern for our fellows. We're self-reliant, yet not in the extreme. We know when to pick up the phone to talk a worry over with a friend and when to chew over a dilemma on our own. We're emotionally connected—not loners so bottled up with rage that we're holed up in survivalist caves with killer pit bulls and assault rifles.

Alfred Adler, the renowned psychotherapist, believed that mature psychological development integrates us socially and occupationally and that it also welcomes proper intimacy. I say the wholesomely autonomous are open to the sublime nuances of the Spirit in everyday life.

Wholesome autonomy is the zenith of psychological health that ushers in a robust spirituality (and vice versa). With a wholesome independence we tend to advance the well-being of others, not only our own. That too we manage in our own way.

Contemplatives Need Trusted Counselors Too

Competent spiritual guidance may be in order, no matter what lifestyle we choose. Wholesome autonomy, in and of itself, could well require therapy, for surely the good life is also well examined. If we feel called to silence and solitary disciplines, a trusted spiritual director—someone who knows about and appreciates the contemplative journey—can help us sort out our critical paring-downs. Let's hope we can avoid those efficiency-driven counselors who adore quick-fix cures, and are inhospitable to the fertile aimlessness of contemplation. If I were choosing a therapist or a spiritual director today, I'd search for someone who *lives* contemplatively, someone who places direct transcendent experience, even faith, at the core—not at the periphery—of psychological health, and someone with a good sense of humor about practically everything.

As we scale back our social life or step up an enterprise, we'll probably need to unburden ourselves to a knowledgeable counselor. We can evaluate our readiness for that by checking our emotional pulse once in a while. For example, what have you felt thus far reading these pages? Sad? Glad? Bored? Bewildered? Discontented? Desirous? Intense feelings are red flags warning us to stop and pay attention. Pain, fear, the apathy or lopsidedness of our life, even our dreams can reveal the costs of vain pursuits or a frenetic pace. The quality of our subjective life points to what we need by way of self-renewing routines.

There are elementary tasks. One early step is to compare meditation methods. Not all practices are alike. If we read, study, or attend various lecture programs, contrasts are obvious. We can follow that up with subsequent assessment talks with an experienced, reliable practitioner. Each meditation teacher necessarily believes his or her technique and spiritual heritage is best. Some methods are linked to religious practices that we may not wish to adopt. Once, in a flurry of excitement over a meditation program, I gave my mother a gift certificate for initiation in the popular approach. She thanked me for the present, attended one introductory lecture, then phoned me in horror over the religious overtones, which she was convinced were of the devil. Who knew?

Then too, in our competitive, industrialized climate the meditative arts are now Big Business. It's in some schools' best economic interest to initiate you, enroll you in programs, and sell you oodles of tapes and training systems. However, your initial goal is to evaluate what's best for *you*. The nuances of this issue are so subtle and significant that I'll revisit the topic later.

Another early step involves observing your experience. When one woman decided to leave her well-paying, professional position for another career, she felt profoundly anxious. She realized she was financially wedded to her job. That marriage was made in Hell, and she wanted a divorce. She resisted. Rather than air out her unhappy feelings by talking with a therapist, she pooh-poohed her mounting fears. Her discomfort intensified. Then one night she had the following dream:

> I had died and was moving into my home in the afterlife—a drab, dingy, and utterly impoverished space—like a rat-infested, decaying tenement. A man in

a brilliant white suit knocked on my door. He had come to look in on me—to make sure I had arrived safely. Anyway, I asked him, "What is this horrible place? Why am I not in the beautiful house I'm used to?" and he replied, "Oh, this is the house you built while you were alive as you invested your faith in treasures that rot. Now all that rust is a witness against you."

The chilling message of future pain in that dream was stirred by her scriptural studies, and disturbed this woman more than the prospect of therapy. Her dream's troubling image reflected the obvious: although she feared economic deprivation, her conscience told her that was a costly, short-sighted error. She now felt motivated to tackle her career problems constructively. Subsequent discussions with a qualified counselor revealed that she *knew* that by choosing security over healthful growth she was corrupting her spiritual well-being. Her dream doesn't mean that you or someone else will suffer pangs of guilt when choosing financial security over some sort of growth. It means that *she* did.

The illogic of some dreams graphically reveals what logic hides: our material goals must support our *spiritual* aims. Uncovering those aims is integral to shaping a contemplative, well-integrated life. As discussed earlier, it helps to inject a career or interpersonal objective with the wisdom of our deepest awareness. Without a prayerful underpinning to our efforts, we'll eventually agree with Thomas Aquinas that all accomplishments are straw compared to what is revealed to us by God.

Be of good cheer. The unsettling summons to lead a life

of sacred, "right relationship" comes with its own built-in promise of fulfillment. As it is written in Psalm 91: The Lord "shall give his angels charge over thee, to keep thee in all thy ways."

Shaping Contemplative Life

Two acquaintances with a contemplative bent live vastly different lives. I'd call them both wholesomely autonomous. They sustain their spiritual integrity and their workaday composure in the face of what might otherwise be overloads of feverish activity. One seems to prefer partial solitude and the stillness of nature. The other has a flair for leadership and worldwide adventure. Each exhibits what some call "right giving"—the constructive, authentic use of gifts and predilections. Each adds value to the lives of others in a distinctive way.

One acquaintance is a neighbor I'll call Pete. (That's not his real name.) During the week Pete works and lives in a whitewashed, one-room cottage. Every Friday he drives two hours south to his family home to spend the weekend with his wife and children. Pete is quiet and dependable—a good provider, faithful and hardworking. He supports his kids through college. He escorts his wife to jazz festivals by the river in the summer. She's a musician of sorts, and on weekends and holidays the two of them routinely party with a crowd of old, good friends at cookouts and Indian restaurants in San Francisco. Pete repairs his roof when it leaks. He visits his aging parent regularly. He's also a cheerful curmudgeon—one of the householder variety of the species "casual contemplative." Pete is not overtly spiritual. I've never heard him speak of God or meditation or his "inner child." He does, however, dote on his time alone, reveres living in the woods, takes long walks by the beach, and loves nature's silence. He uses electronic gadgets while at work but spurns e-mail, faxes, and computers when he's at home. He won't tolerate these voices of intrusion in his cottage and sees no reason to install a phone.

Pete's been phoneless since I've known him. That seems to be his chief luxury. He doesn't ask much more for himself, but swears that *not* talking for a spell is one of his "good health" secrets:

> *My friends ask, "How can you exist without a phone?" Then they list all the reasons why I should install one. Well, I'm happier this way. My wife knows how to reach me in case of an emergency. I unwind in my own way. After eight hours at work, it's soothing to cook dinner while listening to Chico Hamilton. I eat and then read in silence—knowing I won't be interrupted by telemarketers or chatty friends.*

With no expert instruction, and on his own, Pete has cultivated a contented, listening heart—"the hearing ear and the seeing eye" extolled in Proverbs 20. I've concluded that he knows how to attend inwardly as the prophet Isaiah (30:21) instructs: If we're aware, we can hear that small still voice saying, *This is the way. Walk ye in it.*

My second acquaintance is a senior-level helping professional. I'll call her U.N. She works full-time, and then some, in a fairly regimented corporate environment. U.N. serves on numerous statewide committees. She writes and edits professional newsletters and articles. She organizes public events, serves as an adviser on nonprofit boards, and is active in her church. She's also a world traveler. During the last year alone U.N. journeyed to New Zealand, Mexico, the United Kingdom twice, and Paris three times. She thinks nothing of boarding a jet on a Friday red-eye, meeting a traveling companion in New York early on Saturday morning, and flying off to London or France for a week.

U.N. begins each day by meditating at dawn for about thirty minutes. She meditates at home, on airplanes, at business conferences. Despite the heavy demands on her time, U.N. says she feels collected because she starts each day serenely:

> *I shower, drink one cup of coffee, then go into my den and meditate with TM for thirty minutes. It organizes me.*

> *I work hard, yet feel easy inside—no rush to judgment about things. No self-pressure. No doubts when someone else criticizes me. That's my twenty-five-year habit, and like my Amex card, I never leave home without it.*

Pete and U.N. prove that a casually contemplative life can be cultivated outside a monastery. The life is largely attitudinal, not doctrinal. Neither follows a lockstep spiritual recipe formulated by some expert. Neither lives in *absolute* seclusion. Both are contributive and loving—in their own way. Each employs stillness and solitude discerningly, in the service of daily life. They may not be actively seeking what the mystics call union with God, but then again, who knows what's really lodged in anyone's secret heart? U.N. and Pete aren't stringently ascetic. That is, neither is a monk in the way I use the term in chapter 1. Still, each honors a unique spiritual fingerprint and has devised idiosyncratic means to pursue a special depth of inner experience—meaningful spiritual comfort.

IDEAS FOR THE SPIRITUAL WALK

Customize Your Prayer Habit

We don't exactly "deserve" spiritual well-being. It's unmerited, like grace itself. Ax murderers, pickpockets, smarmy lawyers, and slippery investment bankers are all prime candidates for the Spirit's intercession. So are we. One need only put oneself in a room—on a bed, in a chair, on the floor—and quiet the mind. Breathing follows suit. Positive expectancy, that listening and gazing inward, leads to prayer *in* the Spirit. The Spirit within—not our sterling character—activates the healing and lessens discord. All we need to do is establish a sincere prayer *habit* to *un*stimulate ourselves. Best of all, we can customize that practice just about any way we want.

In the early 1900s Murial Lester "influenced multitudes" in the uniqueness of their devotional life. She pointed out the link between an unfussy, silent sitting and deep prayer and made the following suggestions:

- Let your minimum be twenty minutes a day spent practicing the presence of God.
- Twenty minutes given to adoration, joy, thanksgiving, meditation, and intercession.
- This praying time could be spent sitting, kneeling, lying, walking, whichever one finds more apt.
- It could be split up into fractions of time or taken in a single period.
- Thus one would acquire the habit of facing events objectively.
- Thus would one's mind become clarified by the habit of thinking in the presence of God.[7]

Step 1: Cooperate with Your Current Schedule

To follow Lester's ideas faithfully is to develop a decent devotional life. Your increased serenity will accommodate your obligations and your rhythms of high and low energy. Look to your chosen spiritual heritage for methods of praying in the Spirit. What's the motif of your spiritual fingerprint? Are mornings your worst times? Well then, honor your nights.

Step 2: Consider a Contemplative Ritual Before Sleep

If it suits you, try this: Prop yourself up in bed. Brace your neck and back with sturdy pillows. Get comfy. Pick a time when the house is dark and still—after you've turned off Leno or Letterman and everyone else is asleep.

If your toddler has a bad dream and crawls into bed beside you, if your Siamese cat curls up purring by your side, so much the better. Just cradle in your arms any-one—or anything—cuddling close by. With a prayerful heart, your hallowed mental climate will envelop those who are in your midst. Then close your eyes and repeat a favored word or psalm.

Relax into your words and breath. Don't force your breathing to match the tempo of your inward speech. That may occur quite naturally. *Don't force anything.* Should you fall asleep during your silent sitting, no problem. This is not precisely a meditation in which, when you doze off, sleep may be an avoidance of the process. On the other hand, "sleep-prayer" is one of the finest forms of repose known to humankind. You'll be blessed as you sleep. Over time you'll gain the power to stay awake while praying. (Don't forget: "The joy of the Lord *is* your strength.") Your Immortal Eyes could stay open all night; even as your body sleeps, your deepest mind entertains some holy thought if you "meditate in the night watches." (Ps. 63:6).

If you doubt that prayer and slumber could combine, reflect on Psalm 4, especially at bedtime:

Meditate in your heart upon your bed, and be still. . . .
In peace I will both lie down and sleep,
For thou alone, O Lord, dost make me to dwell in safety.

3

A Distinctive Reflection of Oneness

Behold, thou desirest truth in the inward parts, and in the hidden part thou shalt make me to know wisdom.

—Psalm 51:6

Living in society was essential to Dietrich Bonhoeffer's spiritual completion. Only by engaging completely with this world could he acquire strong faith.[1] John Muir left society for the woods. Gandhi bade good-bye to both society and carnal pleasure so that a deeper love might infuse his intimacies with his wife. Yet Gandhi led a mixed life. In South Africa he kept to himself as a solitary while he functioned as a householder, politician, lawyer, and social reformer. In India too, Gandhi's conscious choice to live "the lonesome way" was deliberate, "necessary in response to the calls of public duty."[2]

Some people are spiritual introverts. Others are outgoing—their spiritual distinctiveness involves added degrees of social activism. Many are somewhere in between. Living well spiritually necessitates awakening a recollected awareness, and heeding the "small still voice" that animates vital life.

Spiritualities come in all shapes and sizes, and it's critical to understand one's own. If we strain to mimic a Bonhoeffer, a Muir, a Mother Teresa, or a Gandhi, we forfeit our own law of being, our own vital life. Rephrasing Saint Francis de Sales's motto, "*Be* who you are and be that perfectly," we find a cornerstone on which to build a casually contemplative life. One thing is clear: an awakening individual discerns what's needed, knows when enough of one activity is enough, and demonstrates that deeper knowing.

Vital life flourishes every which way. It cascades like living water from our being, from our gifts, and the way in which we're called out, spiritually, to complete ourselves as individuals in the scheme of community. That calling-out is a vocation, and, whatever else they may be doing, contemplatives are summoned to that reflective life. We've seen that we can adapt a contemplative prayer habit and its disciplining routines to our preferred lifestyle. With interior peace comes a more rigorous self-renewal. That thrust ultimately empowers our life with others, which must be why leadership expert John Gardner called self-renewal a leader's most important task. Proper renewal lets us extend our reach, but only in our own way. By knowing ourselves as spiritually *unique,* we can, at some point, convert our entire life to honor our inmost calling.

Prayer, meditation, and even diverse physical disciplines are useful. The slow, balletlike exercises of the Pilates method or brisk race-walking both can help us grow whole in a manner worthy of our summons. Depending on our temperament, various contemplative practices are potentially liberating. If we cultivate an intuition about what specific disciplines might lift us out of ourselves, and begin to practice these, we turn our attention toward Truth, thereby increasing the probability of true healing or wholeness.

Each One is Spiritually Intelligent

Each of us is born with a one-of-a-kind spirituality. That means we're animated into a vital life idiosyncratically.[3] On all scores of the heart, we grow closer to God *only* if we honor what elsewhere I've called our spiritual intelligence. That's our intuitive, inspired thought, and our fingerprint of soul.[4]

In *Zen Spirit, Christian Spirit,* Robert Kennedy tells the story of an orphaned child who lived with monks "in a monastery far away": "Jesus appeared to the little boy and held him in his arms. When the monks came upon this scene, they heard Jesus ask the little boy, 'Marcellino, do you know who I am?' The little boy, with childlike faith, answered, 'Yes.'"[5]

There's a lesson here for us. When we pray, we only need to greet our God in that same spirit of childlike trust. Let's keep this matter of contemplation simple. Let's stay real. Our practice is designed to open our eyes, to see that "the very pebbles sparkle."[6]

We are as diverse in our spirituality and prayer-life as dancers, herbalists, architects, and diesel mechanics are in their vocations. Nevertheless, an inspired dancer knows an inspired architect when he meets her. He empathizes with her. They're on the same wavelength of creative expression. Or excellence radiates through each one's work. We too can resonate with others' spirituality by respecting the dialect they use to describe whatever animates their life. The metaphysicians don't verbalize their spiritual experience in the same way as the fundamentalists, who don't speak of God in the same way as most mystics, who tell of their interior life in somewhat different terms from the naturalists, who don't view the things of God exactly like the social reformers in the crowd. Meister Eckhart saw that as much as we are in God, so much in peace we are. In his poem "suppose," e. e. cummings saw Life as an old man carrying flowers on his head. John Muir saw his "way to the Universe through a forest wilderness." So God *is* peace, *is* an old man with a pot on his head, *is* a forest wilderness—wild and untamable—all that and more. Mary Baker Eddy called God All in All, and said whatever blesses one blesses all. Just so: we may perceive distinctively, but whatever blesses you will, ultimately, bless me. Truth is Truth. The blessed apprehend Truth in anything they view, "and all of us are the work of Thy hand" (Isaiah 64:8).

A Johnny Appleseed may swoon over lichen-covered apple trees and tender green saplings. Someone like the poet Rainer Maria Rilke or the mystic Evelyn Underhill may rhapsodize about a poem, a psalm, the koan of a revered

Zen master. Others, whether window washers, gymnasts or gardeners, may follow their own prodigious wisdom to spiritual illumination. Some of us have a spiritual intelligence that seems almost kinesthetic. But few talk of that.

When that wizened clockmaker-turned-healer P. P. Quimby was dying of consumption, traditional medicine was killing him. He needed something new, the change of scene that stirs a fresh perspective. He trekked over miles of dirt road to find it, describing the prelude to his journey this way: *"I became so low that it was with difficulty I could walk. . . . I had taken so much calomel that my system was said to be poisoned with it; and I lost many of my teeth . . . and my liver [and kidneys were] diseased."*[7]

Quimby "gave up to die." Then he remembered that an acquaintance cured himself by riding horseback. Since he was too weak to ride, Quimby chose to get out into the fresh air in a horse-drawn carriage. Far from home, his horse suddenly stopped trotting, wouldn't walk, refused to budge. Forced to seek assistance on foot, Quimby soon forgot himself. He began to run. Ignoring his condition, he ran for miles, up hills and down until at last, exhausted, he found help *and* his healing. Quimby's cure seems to have been total.

In Quimby's case—not necessarily in ours—healing was triggered by *physical* exertion. That walk, those miles, the sheer hardship of it, the intense bodily stimulation blew Quimby's mind. Incomprehensibly, his awareness shifted as his thoughts were lifted above circumstance in that wholly converting, revitalizing fashion that Scripture demands: "He who would save his life must first lose it."

Contemplatives Seek Metanoia

It's that complete loss of self, or "self-vanishing," that contemplatives seek. Not doctrinal debate. Not academic theories. The conversion experience of spiritual illumination is metanoia—the total restructuring of personal reality through the total regeneration of body, mind, and spirit. That transformation includes healthy, if often unsettling, growth. We feel ambitious where previously we felt torpor. Or we decide to take another chance at love where, before, we guarded our heart. Growth leaves us feeling off-kilter. Something feels different, but what? We have the same feeling Alice in Wonderland had when, all turned around, she experiences "a very curious sensation—which puzzled her until she made out what it was": she is growing again.[8] Alice is shifting in physical size. A spiritual conversion is largely subjective. It upsets, then settles, us on the inside, once and for all. Yet that course correction can feel strange because the "outside" world morphs into something boundless and brand new.

With Quimby's reformation came endless insight and the miracle of restored health. Constricting beliefs fell away. Obedience to the reasonable cautions of a consensus viewpoint evaporated. Quimby could now afford to bypass the medical predictions of his early demise. An unqualified inner certainty pronounced him healed. I speculate that his change of mind flourished as he forgot the "world of the personal"—the material world. Strenuous exercise seems to have given Quimby the subjective means to enter a sparkling, superior reality. Constant physical movement may have advanced his spiritual wisdom. I say "may have" because no one really knows *how* miracles work. As Kathryn Kuhlman, the world-reknown faith healer, said, "A doctor has the power and ability to set a bone, but he must wait for Divine power to heal."[9] Our healings come by grace, out of time, and quicker than the blink of an eye.

Our favored spiritual realities could assist our radical healings, our own conversion. A few people know exactly how to pay attention to their spiritual wisdom. They listen and listen—to taped talks, to sermons, to chance remarks, to lectures, to song lyrics—for their inner lift. Some bend and stretch their bodies to arrive at the still point within that has no beginning and no end. Some pray and pray without ceasing, as did that anonymous, beleaguered seeker in *The Way of the Pilgrim* who repeated the Jesus Prayer a zillion times a day. Maybe you're one who must read and study and cogitate in order to gain wholeness of mind, body, and spirit.[10]

Emma Curtis Hopkins, a mild-mannered schoolteacher turned metaphysical-dynamo, seems to have exemplified that scholarly pattern. First she studied Eastern philosophies extensively, on her own. Then she joined Mary Baker Eddy, becoming engrossed with Eddy's ideas. Hopkins's mind was ablaze with spiritual truths. After leaving Eddy, it is said that she became a powerful, unobtrusive mentor to many future leaders of the New Thought movement of the early 1900s, such as Ernest Holmes, founder of the Science of Mind Church, and Charles and Mildred Filmore, cofounders of the Unity School of Christianity.[11]

Spiritual Diversities

Once I heard a dancer say, "Every step I take is quick and lively—my choreography reflects my nervous system."

Saint Francis seems to have been that sort of live wire, except, says G. K. Chesterton, he was God's hoofer, thread-thin, and "vibrant as a bowstring." Francis's insights pierced the veil of convention like arrows.[12] Compare Francis to Saint Thomas Aquinas, a placid, clunky plodder nicknamed "the Dumb Ox." Slow. Sober. Distracted. Aquinas found his spiritual way through profound contemplation—not pirouettes of mind—in the middle ground of facts "given by the senses" where "reason has a right to rule, as a representative of God in Man."[13] Spirituality has no one face or form. Its manifestations are infinite.

With brutal honesty, Barbara Wilson cuts through the chaff of her spiritual likes and dislikes. She knows herself. She is a good teacher who illustrates the honesty and self-awareness we all need to individualize a contemplative life or achieve any spiritual victory. In *Blue Windows,* Wilson explains why some types of spiritual discussions weigh her down:

> *I am not at home in the upper realms of speculative thought. I have never had a metaphysical mind, not as a child, and not now. I am comfortable with ideas, but ideas that are closer to home, ideas that are based on particulars, on specifics. Most of all I like the particulars themselves. I like things I can see and touch, taste and hear and smell. I have always liked them best.*[14]

By contrast, others feel right at home in the "upper realms of speculative thought." Since early childhood, my preferred musings have included long, strong drinks of abstract thought. As an adult, mystical prose—like that of Evelyn Underhill, Julian of Norwich, and the contemplative-mystics Abhishiktānanda, Thomas Merton, and Raimon Panikkar—has engaged me. I can (and routinely do) spend hours imbibing metaphysical ideas. Lengthy narratives about sensory things sometimes strike me as a bit too precious, too finely crafted and thus tedious. Just a dash, please.

My point is that spiritual distinctiveness permeates our every proclivity: how we enjoy using our mind; how we prefer to work; how we best relate; how we pray. This last item is so crucial to spiritual progress, so sorely overlooked in the spiritual literature, that we'll return to the topic later.

We block our spiritual progression if, like little plastic robots, we indiscriminately copy someone else's prayer method just because it's easy and available and predigested. Our spiritual intelligence reveals our fingerprint of soul. That print involves encountering our inherent talents and inclinations. We can ask, "What brings me to life? When am I most alive?"

One individual prays while moving her body—*because* she is born to whirl or run fast or practice aikido or play the drums. Here, other traditions, like the Sufi and Native American, may have much to teach us, for the role that kinesthetics plays in releasing *spiritual* intelligence is badly neglected in Western culture. Another individual sips of pure living water while singing in a choir. Another prays in the Spirit while quilting. Some mix of prayerful techniques could be ideal for us. Our fingerprint of soul, not convention or a chilly intellect, should determine what "form" of prayer we foster:

> For example, in Buddhism, the Obaku sect combines zazan with nembutsu (the invocation of the name Amida). . . . Even today there are so-called Zen Christians who practice Zen while reciting the name of Christ in place of the name of Amida. During the Meiji era there were outstanding Christians who recited the Our Father while striking the mokugyo (a wooden block that marks the rhythm in Buddhist prayers). . . . What is essential and universal is the common element of "total concentration in prayer."[15]

Your way of praying in the Spirit will not necessarily mirror your brother's or your mother's or mine. The exercises in this book undoubtedly indicate that I favor a Westernized and Christian contemplative prayer, including meditation and reflecting on Scripture. For me, God's Word is alive with power, and as I ingest that Word I am enlivened too. Even so, Hindu (mantra) methods and the Buddhist practice of attending to the breath have seeped into my routines.

I've heard it said that intellectual types favor observation methods, such as in Zen-style meditations, while more emotional individuals prefer mantra methods. One contemplative expert will extol TM or some other mantra-type program. Another will swear to you that the mantra dulls awareness and that the genuinely holy will intuitively reject that approach. A Fundamentalist Christian, for instance, is unlikely to practice yoga or chanting, since these disciplines have Eastern roots. On the other hand, some chanters probably feel right at home when praying in the Spirit. So what's a novice to do? How to proceed? Repeating an earlier suggestion, it helps to consult an unbiased, experienced expert—or several—while assessing what's best for us. It may turn out that we'll choose to mix our disciplines.

Since God is always *beyond* any one form of prayer, our devotions must yield to our inherent spirituality if we want unitive remembrance. A consciousness of Oneness "can drink from the stream at its very sources, from those true and essential waters. Here the water is sweet and fresh and pure, as every stream is sweet at its source, before it has lost its cool freshness and purity."[16]

Each of us recollects the Light that *is* our life along a slightly individualized route. Jacob had his illuminative dream. Saul, who later became Paul, was struck dumb and blind while trudging down a dusty road. (Shades of P. P. Quimby?) Rumi the Sufi mystic had his mentor, Shams of Tabriz, who led him by example and personal encouragement to love. Here's my point: there's only one overarching Truth that leads to abundant, everlasting Life. Yet it's possible that diverse voices, teachers, and experiences can open our eyes to see, and our ears to hear.

Contemplatives Seek Mystical Meanings

Years ago I knew a thoughtful, morally elevated man. He was married, retired, and affluent. He golfed every weekday. You might say golf turned him on spiritually. The golf course was his sanctuary. Maybe golf was his prayer. Each morning, leaving his house, he'd call out to his wife, "See you later. I'm going to the office." Then he'd stroll across the street to the golf course (his office). For hours each Monday through Friday, he'd amble over acres of greens, lugging golf clubs, bantering with pals, envisioning his next shots and the grand, mysterious movement of life. He was the first casual contemplative I'd ever known, yet a more disciplined intent I've rarely encountered.

My friend was not religious—he was no churchgoer, no fan of anything organized, and no joiner of groups. He was *spiritual*. In him I sensed a hunger for life lived full out, with truthfulness and overarching passion. Apparently in golf he found a contemplative discipline that led to more abundant life, quite possibly one with mystical meaning.

Michael Murphy views the game of golf through a similarly transcendent filter. To Murphy, golf symbolizes life's spiritual motion, for he writes, surely we are progressing toward something: "There is no escaping the long march of our lives: that is part of the reason people reenact it again and again on the golf course, my golfing teacher said. They are working out something built into their genes."[17]

Why can't golfers and quilters and grocery clerks be considered saintly, if they measure up? That's how I picture Harvey Penick, the legendary golf teacher—as saintly, certainly as a life lover. Only saints and life lovers demystify spirituality, and encourage us to be true-blue to ourselves. Penick always taught his students to be authentic, no matter what else seemed to be going on:

> *[Before an important game] do as you usually do. If you ordinarily have a couple of drinks in the evening, do it. If*

you have been going to bed at 11 P.M., do not crawl between the sheets two hours earlier than normal. . . . You must understand that it is your mind that will have the most to do with how you play in the big match.[18]

Exactly.

So back to spiritual fingerprints: What brings you to life? How do *you* love to use your mind? When left to your own devices, how do you learn best? What activities, normal doings, or spiritual dreams give you a lift? Your deepest mind will tell you secrets and can reveal how you're inclined to pray in the Spirit, heal, love, and be most alive. That information comes with contemplative alertness. Ultimately it's your own attention that unsettles you or puts you at ease.

Contemplatives *Flourish* in Stillness

As degrees of solitude or separation from society differ, so do degrees of interior stillness. Those who love silence wholesomely love the Presence that *is* Silence—not the legalism of their life. A laid-back, trusting stillness depends on consciously turning toward Truth—getting established in the very nature of God while rejecting the blind following of laws: "For, on the one hand, there is a setting aside of a former commandment because of its weakness and uselessness (for the Law made nothing perfect), and on the other hand there is a bringing in of a better hope, through which we draw near to God" (Hebrews 7:18–19).

If we feel uniquely drawn to that sort of silence, we may

identify with Julian of Norwich, who lived in a tiny room, a cage of sorts. A physical cell enabled her absolute freedom. She blessed her earthly solitude while using it to bless *us*. In contemplative stillness, like Julian, we can flourish, can realize with Julian that joy, more than sorrow, guilt, or gravity, affirms the structure—the deepest underlying nature—of the Lord:

> The blessed woman saw God in many ways,
> but she saw him take his rest nowhere but in man's soul;
> his will is that we rejoice more in his love than we sorrow
>   over our frequent falls.[19]

Or we may admire the more socially-active courage of Saint Clare, who with her small band of spiritual companions gathered in a threadbare Italian cloister at the bidding of her mentor, Saint Francis of Assisi. There, hidden in wordless, contemplative passion, Clare flourished—as did her spiritual leadership over a contemplative order that endures to this day. Two hearty influencers: One in a cell, the other more in the world, both fueled by the Silence that is a Presence.[20]

Contemplatives Enjoy Spiritual Hiddenness

From Clare's spiritual friend Saint Francis, we learn more about a healthy hiddenness. Francis danced with his sister Nature and conversed with the birds, and clung to concealments of a special order—what he called "God's secrets." Once he inquired of his brother friars whether he should publicly disclose a vision he'd had. They counseled him to "tell all." They said that God's secrets to us should be shared with the world. Francis resolved to do exactly the opposite, stating, "It is for me to keep my secrets to myself." He convinced the friars that God had revealed some things to him that he would never divulge as long as he lived.[21]

This seems the illogical tidbit of bullheadedness that preserves a contemplative's sanity, and even ensures blessings. The rule about keeping *some* things to ourselves reflects another ethereal nuance of stillness about which G. K. Chesterton knew plenty. He wrote that in fairy tales "You may live in a palace of gold and sapphire, *if* you do not say the word 'cow'" or utter certain other words. Or "You may live happily with the King's daughter, *if* you do not show her an onion."[22] The rewards we seek always hang upon conditions. As noted in the introduction, there's a catch to our turning-of-mind. Contemplative life demands discretion. *If* we don't spill the beans of our sacred communion, we grow from it.

It's so easy to degrade our profound understandings. First we trivialize spiritual experience by chattering of it indiscriminately. Then too, as Merton cautioned, the true emptiness that contemplatives seek can*not* be described: "It is not this; it is not that." Furthermore, "whatever you say of it, it is other than what you say."[23] "Go and tell no one," was Jesus' watchword when healing almost anyone. He spoke to the multitudes with one voice but used another for his intimates. There's information here— instruction for those who feel alienated when speaking of spiritual growth with certain friends or family. In most cases, that's a *self* setup. By saying too much, we court misunderstanding. Perhaps we do so to feel superior or different.

Even those closest to Jesus weren't ready to grasp all his meanings. He held back, telling his disciples, "I have many more things to say to you, but you cannot bear them now" (John 16:12). When it comes to bearing anything profound—especially the "good life" or our "beams of love"—there's lots of maturing needed.

Theologian Paul Tillich defined the good life as life ever surpassing itself. To surpass ourselves spiritually, wherever we are now, we have to curb our speech. No one is too busy for that practice. In fact, the busiest people—and the most materially successful—often do that best. Reserve is wholly contemplative. It requires focus, self-control, and discipline. For although the tongue is "a little member" (James 3:5) within our body, it is fully capable of defiling the course of our life.

The good life is our vital life. Dallas Willard emphasizes it is available only if we consciously adopt the habits and deportment that prepare mind and body to be radically restored. We can borrow our disciplines of prayer, meditation, and fasting from the contemplative tradition.[24] We can evolve our devotional practices out of what's tried and true and in line with our heritage of choice. We can combine methods. We can do all that to reorient ourselves completely toward Love, but *not* to make a god of asceticism or to torment ourselves into a guilty, double-minded, brittle holiness. Contemplative health demands surrender to our right mind, our mind of Love and intimate, right relationship with the indwelling Spirit. *That's* what changes us, restores and renews our consciousness—not discipline per se.

Contemplatives Let the Spirit Lead

My own contemplative life involves an ambling art of worship. It's intuitive. I'm a meanderer, a zigzagger. I tend to embrace my failings rather than whip myself into an alienated lather of self-improvement schemes. I feel, like Muir, that transcendental daydreaming is fundamental, essential, the substantial enterprise of life.[25] External drivers of my time have lost their power, and I am no longer an adrenaline junkie. That's too distracting. Instead of imposing *my* pictures of achievement too forcibly on a weekly schedule, I trust that small, still inner voice to nudge me through my day. Come to think of it, God *is* my flowering day.

I still concoct a "to do" list each morning, and still plan corporate and project outcomes for the fiscal year, for the four quarters, and for each month and week. That's only tidy. It's businesslike—the soundness behind Baltasar Gracián's command to parcel things out wisely. But I pretty much chip away at things as the Spirit—not the list—moves me. This custom gives me back the day.

I also like to put those sorts of ideals into everyday use. What good is it, I ask myself, if I'm all calm and smooth after church on Sunday, but afterward, while speeding back home, feel like rear-ending the bumper of a plodding driver? If it's right relationship with God we're seeking, we'll set our face like flint to *reflect* that peace in our normal doings. That's our human challenge and our discipline: it takes thought and steadfast focus to bridle the tongue and to smooth out the stony places in ourselves that choke comfort or vitality from our life.

Elsewhere I've written that a spiritual director once called mine a "mixed life." She added that this pattern of living is active and contributive, yet rich with reflective nondoing. I felt heard, respected—as if, for the first time, someone sensed what I genuinely wanted and embraced that as possible for me. My own life-style choices came only with time and considerable thought. All through the years while I was learning what makes me tick spiritually, that woman's words edified me. Despite secular engagements like lectures or the somewhat steady press of corporate projects, today my own mix of prayerful methods and "nondoing" days fosters a life hidden in Christ.

Spiritual existence seems intimate and distinct. Soul is a veritable prayer, comprising an eternity of unfolding epiphanies and rejoicing, private insights. The Book of Matthew (6:6) warns us: There *are* secrets we should keep. The saintly Baltasar Gracián also counsels us on this: "Not all truths can be spoken: Some should be silenced for your own sake, others for the sake of someone else."[26] Whatever whorls we find in our spiritual fingerprint, we may not be able to explain them so easily. In this, even our most intimate disclosures require discernment.

IDEAS FOR THE SPIRITUAL WALK

Encountering Spiritual Uniqueness

John Gardner, author, leadership theorist, and social activist, suggested that a leader's most creative task is self-renewal. Those of us who seek a deeper harmony in life first have to get in touch with how we, as distinctive individuals, maximize our creativity. Creativity, self-renewal, and spiritual uniqueness are linked.

Ideas flow readily when we are *mentally* relaxed. Motivation, productivity, and self-renewal are enhanced when our goals are a *little* difficult but not too far out of reach. It makes sense to loaf in our favorite way, to identify the activities that restore us. Swimming laps at the YMCA may send your brother into the ethers of enjoyment but leave you cold. A foot massage, aromatherapy, or a week at the Golden Door spa could be your relaxation ideal. Do what you love—not only in work but in leisure too.

Temperament, our overall belief system, and our obligations set the terms for relaxation. If we feel guilty when we're not buzzing around like busy bees, it helps to remember that the true self is goal-*less*, and delights in abundance (Isaiah 55).

Step 1: Ask Spiritual Questions

Plan your time off. Walks on the beach, playing ball with your child, enjoying solitude on red-eye flights to distant business meetings are situations that can help us unwind. At such times we ponder the sidebar questions nibbling at awareness that relate to our vital life:

- What's worth doing?
- What obligations do I love (or resent) most, and why?
- How do I most enjoy spending my free time?
- With whom do I most enjoy spending my free time? And which archetypes reliably stimulate my vision of spiritual possibilities?
- In youth, what far-off ideals turned me on, gave me hope, and what do those reveal about my spiritual fingerprint?
- Under what conditions am I most completely engaged or relaxed or likely to enter that optimal creative or spiritual zone some call transcendence or "flow"?
- Under what conditions am I most likely to experience "a distinctive reflection of Oneness"?

Step 2: Reserve Quiet Time

After identifying your preferred methods of self-renewal, look beyond your utilitarian wish to manage stress or hold your tongue when in the presence of the aunt who taunts you. Spiritual renewal is deeper than all that. It is an organizing function. To know yourself, to pray in the Spirit, you'll need quiet times. Paraphrasing Saint John of the Cross, for a little while each day keep yourself apart for one thing only—that which brings everything else with it.

4

A Holy Untangling

I relieved his shoulder from the burden,
His hands were freed from the basket.

—Psalms 81:6

A friend with grown children runs a hectic advisory service. She wakes up at dawn. With a cup of coffee in hand, she spends the first part of each day quietly—praying and reading a verse of Scripture. She loves to write, so follows up her reading by composing a few lines of poetry. Her routine rarely varies. A salesman told me he prefers another routine: the evening—before sleep—is his chosen time for spiritual reflection. I've heard about a neighbor who gazes out of her picture window into the bordering forest for an hour or more *each* afternoon. These three are neither excessively ascetic nor lukewarm about their reflective practices. They are informally dedicated. That commitment makes all the difference.

We begin a contemplative day by setting a watch over our heart. Ideally we spend some time alone, following the rule that God gave Moses: Be ready in the morning, come up, "present thyself there to Me on the top of the mount. And no man shall come up with thee" (Exodus 34:2–3). How we start the day influences its course. This is essential. Morning prayer is meant for every contemplative.

At certain stages of life, it may seem impossible to take that time in a traditional way. We must be creative. We're cultivating a sense of calm, a disposition of trust and wonder. As each occupation, whether teaching, selling, or parenting, has its own performance rules, so each vocation draws us toward the *telio* or completeness of the unity we seek. That movement makes demands on us, and we can feel torn between opposing commitments. A *casual* contemplative may be developing in ways that are only partially clear. Reconciling our various demands—career, family, spiritual—fulfills that deeper *telio*,[1] as a young working mother explains:

> *I don't have time to meditate when I wake up. I'm usually off and running when the alarm clock rings. Evenings are busy too, getting dinner ready, helping my daughter with her bath, and reading together before she goes to sleep. Really the best time I have to put my attention on God is when I am commuting to work in my car (about forty-five minutes each way). I [listen to] tapes on spiritual topics or music. . . . When traffic is*

jammed, I don't stress out. Surrendering to a traffic jam is true spiritual growth!

We may not pray formally every morning, but if somehow we *awaken* to God's presence at our ground of being, that awakening saturates every activity. Contemplative observance helps us *live* in the Spirit. It changes perception, choices, our responses to others. What begins as enhanced awareness smiles on the whole day. To be informal is not, as has been suggested, to be allergic to "all forms of prayer and asceticism."[2] We're gaining the heart's posture of formal prayer, being touched by the sense that *we* are the ones for whom "light ariseth in the darkness" (Psalms 112:4). We're behaving so that, progressively, light shines. As it does, we respond to that spiritual truth.

Even when we miss the mark of an objective or fear that we lack the wherewithal to prevail over some conflict or backbreaking project, the wrinkles in a problem iron out. Life simplifies. Where once we strained to control each little outcome, we're becoming more accepting, less rigid. Paradoxically, as we gain an intuitive authority, we influence selected outcomes with poise. This is holy untangling. The radiant Presence at the center of existence guides our life. Slowly we realize that it's not exactly by means of our brilliance that triumphs come. An unseen grace orchestrates our affairs. As Saint Theresa de Lisieux noted, the difficulties she was too little to rise above, she passed beneath quite simply.

That spiritual trust is not born of passivity. It's an active, ever-attentive stance, exquisitely responsive to life. Formerly we may have set our goals and self-measures according to the standards of a parent, spouse, teacher, or manager. Now a divine, nonlegalistic rule leads our ambitions. We're heeding that influence. In our daily happenings, we may still feel insecure, but we practice "casting our cares" on God, leaning on that Word that promises:

Fear not, for you will not be put to shame;
Neither feel humiliated, for you will not be disgraced. . . .
But with great compassion I will gather you. (Isaiah 54:4–8)

Let's be clear. It is often inconvenient to uncomplicate a fixed worldview, or reorient loyalties, or alter old agreements. We may stall and postpone. Perhaps we've made promises that now we long to break. Waiting for the right time to return to college or to leave one career for another is also tricky. Sometimes the ideal time in the tide of our vital life feels like it's too soon, or too late, or annoying. Imagine driving a Mack truck south to Florida. Suddenly you realize that, to save your life—and maybe the lives of others—you've got to slam on the brakes, navigate a hairpin turn, and head back where you started. You'll have to maneuver your vehicle responsibly to protect everyone's welfare, including your own. Spiritual growth is like that.

In part, it entails paying careful attention to the deepest requirements of Reality. We're learning to live in the world adroitly, consciously, prayerfully, even while maneuvering through all manner of sameness or sudden change. It sounds puzzling. It *is* puzzling. And untold numbers of people manage it. They know their reflective life dignifies them and furthers kindness or, for instance, their ability to tolerate a thankless job and thereby support a family. Or their contemplative life just gladdens them. Abhishiktānanda poetically says that contemplatives who are called to perform some service in the world turn *first* to prayer in order to make society more human: "Prayer is the smile, the friendly glance directed at someone else—maybe a stranger passed on the street . . . —which tells him without saying a word, that to me he is no stranger, but is recognized and loved as a brother."[3]

Anyone—householder, corporate leader, homeless wanderer—can shape a progressively contemplative life with structured, steadying prayer routines. For most of us, prayer is simply responding sweetly, truthfully, rightly at each moment. In essence, that's an issue of *being,* not doing: being more of who we are at our spiritual best, engaging in less of whatever separates us from that recollection.

A pure intent unties knots. I've let many tensions creep into my life by not nipping an obvious discord in the bud. That just requires focus. Imagine the increase of spiritual comfort we'd possess if we attended to an intuition that whispered, "This job, that friend, that investment is not for you." Too often we ignore such cues and then wonder why we feel uneasy. Wholesome growth amplifies the inner directive that says it's time to end a certain career or friendship, or sell our gas-guzzling limo, or get out from under a pile of immobilizing debt. Rather than dissecting our every move or creating a huge melodrama out of revamping some habit, we can simply put first things first—for example, establish a regular time for prayer.

The working mother quoted previously has not

retreated to a mountaintop or to a life of passive quietism. Daily periods of reflection help her sort out priorities. She's a more attentive parent *because* she's calmer. Since it's hard for her to set aside time for the techniques of spiritual growth, she has interpreted her overall role as wife and mother, and its responsibilities, as *spiritual* service, not as thankless tasks or as martyrdom:

> *Spending time with my daughter can be an opportunity for spiritual growth when we really enjoy each other and don't feel rushed to get somewhere or get something done. I know my daughter is a gift from God. She teaches me about . . . wonder and patience. This Saint Patrick's Day she really believed that there'd be a leprechaun inside the "trap" that she and her classmates had made out of boxes at school.*

There are ancient traditions behind all such thinking.

As her child matures it will be easier for this woman to preserve more hours in a day for herself. She already takes classes in the evening at her church and goes on short trips and wilderness retreats alone because her attitude of selfless service is reciprocated at home:

> *My husband belongs to a model railroad club that meets weekly. He has activities occasionally on the weekends. He encouraged me to "get a hobby," which turned out to be . . . classes at my church. My husband isn't a churchgoer, but he fully supports my spiritual growth and steps in to take care of our daughter when I ask him to.*

At first it can be a victory just to *slow down* long enough to save an hour here or there so we can feed ducks at the park. We might read something inspiring, or calming before bed—a text with sacred meaning perhaps, such as a poem, a psalm, or one short proverb. We may pray. After work a busy executive whose home is chock-full of noisy youngsters might sit in his car, collecting his wits and meditating before walking through the front door. A good first rule-of-thumb for a "holy untangling" is to make time for the occasional dawdling that lets us hear a raven's caw and marvel as shadows sweep over pine branches when it sails overhead.

Habits like these cultivate awe and gratitude: "From the rising of the sun unto the going down of the same, the Lord's name is to be praised" (Psalms 113:3).

Intentional Untangling

In effect, casual contemplatives serve their *intentional* goodness. Kierkegaard called that attribute "purity of heart." Should some chore, family request, or social obligation obstruct our deepest intent to be patient or cooperative, we'll know it. We'll *feel* it. We'll acknowledge what needs to be done and move toward it as we are able. If we're rooted in an innocent trust of God, we'll also let things fall into place as unaffectedly and gracefully as possible. Trusting that things will work out, we take action, absorb setbacks, someone's rudeness, our own hypocrisy. We'll rebound after disappointments. Encounter with the deepest dimension of life leaves us optimistic even about loss—say, the death of a loved one. We grieve, but know there's some next level of infinite consciousness; our beloved will live on. With the right confidence, the means for a simpler, more mindful life eventually appear. A little quiet sitting, a routine meditation, a morning yoga class, any of these can produce answers—and the heart to follow through. Pastimes that amused us once no longer do. That in itself frees up huge chunks of time.

After a decent season of meditating or practicing some other contemplative discipline, whatever is contrary to goodness will turn us off. Don't ask me how that works. It just does. For instance, I've often mentioned a friend who has been meditating for years who told me she no longer enjoys violent movies or TV shows: "I still love a good mystery, but not cruelty. And evil is repulsive. So I don't watch much television anymore."

Thomas Merton suggested that the slave in the *spiritual* order robotically obeys the norms and expectations of others. A technology tycoon with a huge fortune of stock holdings can be a spiritual slave, in bondage to the persuasive logic of the marketplace or to stockholders' authority or to "group-think." He or she may feel that an inborn talent doesn't count, could feel riddled with guilt and undeserving of a decent marriage or loyal friends.

Some of us chase after advice from pushy, pretentious experts who themselves chase after what the Bible terms "salutation in the marketplace." Should we fit that chasing profile we'll believe that the conspicuously successful know more than we do, and we reason along these lines: *I'm not rich or famous. Those who are must know the secret to the good life. The worldly-wise and powerful will tell me what to do.*

If we're outgrowing spiritual bondage, we'll know it by our *self*-trust, our self-controls. We'll sense our answers bubbling up from within. Such inner-directedness breeds confidence. Like my friend who's been meditating for years, we'll cast off the dark thoughts, resistances, and choices by which we punish ourselves. Living in a speeded-up culture, we may imagine that this process is quick. Roughly speaking, with things contemplative, the faster we need to go, the *slower* our progress.

Untangling Is Informal

By and large, contemplative living is a peaceable way of being, so relaxed and unvarnished that a little child can appreciate its beauty. If everyday life elevates even an indirect grasp of our spiritual uniqueness, that understanding will eventually untangle us—not by subjecting us to extreme deprivations or ten-step formulas and laundry lists of things to do, but by increasing our sense of who we are. Compassion for our own foibles comes with that untangling. When we live comfortably in our *own* skins, we more easily live with the oddities of others. I'm not saying we'll hang out with everyone who happens along. We'll just accept them.

Every so often, an assortment of straggly wanderers stroll into our area. I'm not sure where they come from. One day they just appear. From their look, they've suffered a trauma—drugs, mental illness, something bad. They walk around town, striding along our dusty, two-lane highway, red bandannas and coattails fluttering in the breeze like wings, trekking from the end of the village to the outskirts of another town miles away. They stop for coffee at the market, sit on a bench, and some argue incomprehensibly with themselves. People treat them politely. For the most part, they're dignified by their visit—or so it seems to me. Then they disappear. Poof. One day here and gone the next.

A few townsfolk say it is a blessing that such visitors spend time here before moving on. That way they've experienced a little peace and respect along their journey.

That example has taught me that a *place*—a hospital, a corporation, an apartment complex, a city neighborhood—can contribute to our informal untangling. Now I notice when communities exert a healing empathy. A collective kindness abounds. In normal times they treat one another well. They don't just theorize about "family values" while crucifying someone who's different. In a crisis people handle things appropriately, as human need dictates, exercising compassion and doing the best that can be done under the circumstance.

Holy Untangling as an Ecstatic Slide

A sage once compared those precious instances of illumination—our "Aha!" moments—to slipping on a banana peel: once we start to slide, matters handle themselves. Suddenly there shines a light from heaven (Acts 9:3). Insights flow from our slides of self-forgetfulness. However magnificent such moments are, they're rare. Furthermore, it's natural to move back and forth between our old loyalties and a sparkling, new spiritual reality.

Some of us feel called to grow within the context of a world of commerce, and some of us feel called to stretch *inwardly*. And if, after all our evolving, we sense it's time to reverse the movement, so be it.

Even the most energetic contemplative will wait for the inner directive that says it's *time* to reach for authentic goals. Whether we're sixteen or sixty-five, we need to hear the small still voice that says, "Get on with it," or we won't press ahead *despite* insecure feelings. We also must heed the cues that whisper, "Hold on. Wait."

The art of life requires knowing which cues to trust and how to sidestep those traps of seductive sentiment related to our illusions of happiness (the sort that says, "Well, I'll just give that old scoundrel another chance—I'm lonely and even if s/he did abuse me in the past . . . "). There's a voice within—still, delicate, faithful—that organizes us, as we'll explore shortly.

If we feel overwhelmed with anger or governed by pressure, the least little habit of meditation can be a tonic.

When a sixty-five-year-old friend started a counseling firm, she felt anxious until she shielded herself from ageist prejudices. On days when she managed to pray and meditate, she could overlook her *own* bias against her age. She also found the strength to ignore the skepticism of others:

> *That taught me a lesson. If I was strong within myself, I was successful—made my sales calls, hooked up with interested clients. My church and a*

small group of like-minded friends supported my illogical ambitions. Each morning I took time to consider my day's goals. I never let myself forget that God is my sacred, ageless Guide.

Slowly fear and doubt lessened. I stopped hanging around with people who fixate on their aches and pains. That's been a steady discipline. A training. Within one year I had a viable business and clients to match.

A refined and gentle executive, contemplative by nature, was fired without warning by his exploitive senior manager. Within that same week the manager coolly invited the executive back to work—temporarily—to complete a complex project. The executive's first reaction was to reject the offer on the spot:

I wanted my manager to know he couldn't do the job without me—wanted him to be hurt, just as I'd been. Then I "heard" the rule: "Love your enemies, bless them that curse you, do good to them that hate you in that ye may be the children of your Father which is in heaven" (Matthew 5:44). That's the word I followed.

His deeper wish was to actualize the charity he truly valued. He didn't *feel* like doing that, but thinking things through calmly and prayerfully, motivated him: "I went back to help out, on my own time. I didn't turn the other cheek to get a reward, but that's how it worked out. In a week that former manager recommended me to a new employer, with rave reviews—his reciprocation for my having turned the other cheek."

That executive wasn't play-acting the role of generous employee. He had tapped into a deep religious intent to discipline his "flesh." For years he'd been learning to control his emotional, *re*active nature, which sought to strike out at anyone who hurt him. This time something clicked. Mulling over his spiritual values, he consciously chose to merge his own thought processes and God's Word about loving others, especially those who "cursed" him.

Chesterton described that integrative love as a paradox demanding contradictory things of us. Either we must pardon unpardonable deeds or we must love unlovable people. Neither act is automatic. Some of our most charitable victories are private and depend on going *against* our feelings. For example, in the workplace we're handed a dozen opportunities each day to practice spiritual generosity.

Whether we're cashiers at Wal-Mart or we've retired to an ornate houseboat, we can experience a mystical self-vanishing if we simplify our *response* to life. Thoughts, speech, conduct—not circumstance—undoes or restores us. Thomas Merton has suggested that our estrangement from our spiritual center—or ground of being—*is* the original sin. We may turn down promotions or aim for a well-paying career. That's not the critical issue. As we train ourselves to honor the spiritual essence beneath everyday life, we know a fulfilling integration, a *mature* spirituality, as our true self. This knowing is absolutely practical. Normal unknowns that could empower us, and make full our joy, are in fact a wisdom revealed by the inner Spirit, as Scripture explains, "For what man knoweth the things of a man, save the spirit . . . which is in him? Even so the things of God knoweth no man, but the Spirit of God" (1 Corinthians 2:9–10).

Holy Untangling Improves Relationships

A contemplative life promotes the self-scrutiny that over time invites new relationships. We're not simply gazing narcissistically at ourselves. We are becoming authentic and therefore capable of service and friendship. People we once overlooked—older, younger, or different culturally—may become our dearest friends.

It's from within our spiritual depths that we're prodded to connect wholesomely to others or leave abusive friends or corrupting work associates. Perhaps we've been too chummy with shallow or codependent family members. We could be self-saboteurs—overly timid people pleasers or ruthlessly self-centered. Who hasn't, from time to time, linked up with unhelpful experts—doctors, lawyers, accountants, and the like? Remarkable associations build when we realize that we can stand up for ourselves in the face of undeserved hostility or rudeness. This in itself is a sign of healthy untangling. Here are two examples.

A semiretired executive with advanced prostate cancer admitted to a corporate focus group that his illness had forced him to reevaluate his conforming existence. For years he had regretted making friends only with men acceptable to his closest circle. His aim in his remaining years was to taste more of life and get to know a wide cross-section of others. He wanted women friends and closer ties with men outside business. Shortly after his disclosure, he joined a new, interfaith church. Its programs included weekly dialogues on spiritual themes, and participants from diverse faiths.

A foursome of friends scattered around the country felt spiritually isolated. Each had a contemplative side. Each had been studying Scripture on her own. The four agreed to conference by phone each month to support the others' growth. One lives in Michigan, one in Tennessee, and the other two in different regions of California. Their dialogue lasted a full year and it cemented a novel, fulfilling form of conversation. During the course of each month they read a short, predetermined passage of Scripture. They jotted down their thoughts for applying those ideas in daily life. During their teleconferences they compared notes. One said of the dialogue, "It was comforting to know that at least once every few weeks I'd feel understood. I also liked hearing how the others were progressing." A second confided that the shared empathy increased her spiritual comfort: "Our discussions lessened the normal alienation of my competitive business life."

Holy Untangling Rounds Us Out

A holy untangling releases actual power. Bit by bit, we experience the vital life that our contemplative disciplines unleash. We see that little things undo or uplift us. We begin to manage hidden strife, like trivial gossip that distracts us from a peaceful mind-set. Even when lazing about, talking on the phone, or lunching with friends, we put our attention to constructive use, observing how we think and talk, use words encouragingly, or speak well about others and ourselves. Our own words and even our smallest tangible acts can gladden us.

Casual contemplatives need not live in monastic confinement. They're all around us—in seashore cottages, gold-gilded condos, and whitewashed lofts. They may be outgoing or introverted. Those who trust their own powers of discernment are likely to distrust a legalistic or institutional spirituality. What's more, the dictatorial spiritual director is a dying breed, a relic of an ultra-authoritarian past.

An elderly farmer and former political aide was referred to me by a poet who knew of my interest in unstructured contemplative life. Long retired from the Washington scene, the farmer now writes poetry. He was wary about granting me an interview and put me on notice: "Don't reveal my whereabouts. A simple life is glorious—especially as one ages—and I for one don't want a horde of writers snooping around, trivializing my beautiful life, framing it in platitudes. An uncluttered, contemplative life is not for people who want to read of it in stylish terms."

Whoever is summoned to a deeply spiritual life is rounded out by actualizing that call to be fully who they are. That's an infinite progression. In time, with persistent contemplative experience, we relinquish our socially-programmed conduct for a vibrant authenticity. That may mean that we:

- *sacrifice* collective opinion, customs, guarantees, or expectations in favor of our core spiritual truths—joy, love, virtue, compassion, beauty, health, and service;
- *sacrifice* unconscious living—not knowing who we are or what we want—in favor of a conscious reflection of the truth of our being;
- *sacrifice* "safe" or acceptable routes of accomplishment in favor of those that may be more demanding, risk-laden, ethical or honest, illogical, unpopular, or unreasonable;
- *sacrifice* our particular risk-avoiding strategies (such as withdrawing from challenge or pretending we can't function) in favor of growing more reliable, committed, responsible, and able.[4]

"Rounding out" means different things to each of us. Initially, reflective routines simply refine our basic humanity. The politico-turned-farmer was exploring a new side of himself when, in his sixties, he moved to the country to raise livestock. Love of privacy and solitude and poetry followed. The executive with prostate cancer discovered a diversity of friendships he had never known before. That's the start of rounding out for him. Who knows where his new associations will lead? Attending to her interior sensibilities, one person learns to complete what she starts. Another admits spiritual lapses: perhaps he's served his family, friends, and corporate managers

selflessly for decades but has ignored God, confining his
devotional life to a measly hour on Sunday. Here again,
state of mind determines the degree to which we'll grap-
ple with our spiritual rounding out. We are, Max Picard
insisted, much better able to endure hostile situations and
people that use us up if we have "the substance of silence
within."[5]

Archetypes and Leaders

The particulars of everyday life reveal our intent. How we
cook a stew, set the table, answer the phone, or treat the UPS
delivery person either improves or undermines the progression of our heart's sacred values. As it's said, "The Spirit lives
in the details."

Gifted spiritual leaders help us define our aspirations.
There are as many ways to grow spiritually as there are
individuals. For someone like the former statesman and
UN peacemaker Dag Hammarskjöld, a contemplative
progression rounded out his life. His contemplative disciplines included keeping a spiritual journal. For more than
thirty-five years, Hammarskjöld recorded the intimate
details of his reflective, religious life in a devotional diary,
later published in part as *Markings*. His outer effectiveness was honed by his inner journey. Hammarskjöld set
down a succession of notes by which we can track the
spiritual development within his professional experience.[6]
At the core we see "at once a reflection, a mirror of the
'public servant' and the 'private man,'" and concurrently

we realize that the Spirit was the prime mover of each facet of Hammarskjöld's life.[7] His diary includes a "jagged" sequence of spiritual growth, despair, and "a 'conversion' in the literal meaning of that word, an 'about-face.'"[8]

In *Markings,* we find a nearly seamless link between Hammarskjöld's private and professional lives. I would not call him casual. Yet his writings do reflect the sensibility of an archetypal contemplative whose reflection and rounding out came from grappling with both his religious feeling and despair. He was not of the world, but his own brand of mysticism helped him function prodigiously *in* it. Despite a "lifelong disdain for conventional society"[9] and what must have been a harried schedule, a public life of constant travel and exacting, high-stakes negotiations, it was possible—no doubt necessary—for Hammarskjöld to protect a deeply spiritual dimension of himself. Urbane, sociable, and sophisticated, he nonetheless lived contemplatively. Why should we, as busy individuals, do less? Leaders know what they need along these lines. They hear some whisper of wisdom within and act on it.

In that vein, once on *Larry King Live* Billy Graham admitted feeling like an occasional failure—as if he hasn't done enough. I felt he was revealing a contemplative longing when he said,

> *I feel that if I had stayed home more, studied more . . . I would have done more for God and my soul. I needed to grow inside more.*

I traveled too much, went too many places, accepted too many invitations . . . and I needed to be preparing so that when I do come and talk [a person senses] something is coming to him that is supernatural.[10]

Several neighborhood couples have shown me what leadership or contemplative success involves. Although ordinary in most respects, these friends have been contemplative pacesetters. One nearby pair arranged their home to give them maximum privacy and holy spaces for daily reflection. These two ex-business friends met, courted, and married at an advanced age—around the time most people retire. As avid meditators, they have created a veritable ashram at home, reserving one bedroom exclusively for yoga and meditation. Having vowed to devote themselves in retirement to these spiritual practices, they've sacrificed vacations, new cars, and other luxuries to that end. Before moving here, I'd never known anyone who valued such a life.

Two favorite friends—now deceased—were self-taught naturalists who lived across the gully. From my deck I could see their yard, could hear them conversing with deer and raccoons. They were composting long before it was in vogue. Everything they did, from mushrooming to cultivating their herb garden, honored the land. Those two had a taste for idleness, for drifting through their grassy chambers, seemingly awestruck by hummingbirds, butterflies, and ferns. They designed their home so that it blended in with the natural colors of the forest. After the redwood boards had weathered, the house was invisible. So is mine, now hidden in a dappled hollow, much to my delight.

The truly spiritual enjoy. They gaze with idiotic plea-sure at this and that, and meet their God everywhere, and realize themselves distinctively.

IDEAS FOR THE SPIRITUAL WALK

Contemplating Holy Untangling

Choose a time and place when you will be undisturbed. Sit in stillness for a few minutes, letting your breathing and mind settle down and become even and "soft." Consider mulling over the following lines for another few minutes, or select a verse you prefer:

> And He was saying, "The Kingdom of God is like a man
>   who casts a seed upon the soil;
> and goes to bed at night and gets up by day, and the seed
>   sprouts up and grows—how, he himself does not know.
> The soil produces crops by itself; first the blade, then the
>   head, then the mature grain in the head.
> But when the crop permits, he himself puts in the sickle,
>   because the harvest has come.
>
> —Mark 4:26–29

- As you reflect on the normal ebb and flow of your life, consider what sort of "seeds" you are now cast-ing upon your ground of being with your thoughts, choices, and aspirations.
- Given your heart's deepest inclination, what "har-vest," or gains, do you desire most? If it would help

your clarity, try writing out your answer in two or three succinct lines. Fine-tune your statement in the weeks to come.

- Given the type and quality of seeds you are currently sowing, what *harvest* do you foresee? What habits might you prefer to start, stop, or monitor?
- Of all the various contemplative practices you've considered lately, what *one* disciplining routine might improve your life's harvest? Your experience of spiritual delight? Why?

5

Learning to Walk Surely

He that walketh uprightly walketh surely . . .

—Proverbs 10:9

Once, against explicit orders to the contrary, and in the middle of the night, I left a desert meditation-sanctuary. Something seemed peculiar. Things didn't *feel* right. Before driving off alone into a pitch-black wilderness, I sat in receptive stillness, wondering what to do. In an instant, I felt what some evangelists call a "scratching on the inside," and a verse from the Book of John popped into my mind: The sheep hear the voice of the good shepherd and follow him, "for they know his voice. And a stranger will they not follow, but will flee from him" (10:4–5).

The group, the place, the rules were, to me, "the stranger." I consciously chose to get out of there. Not that my response should guide anyone else, but that the *princi-*

ple of sitting in receptive stillness—centering oneself in a
Spirit-filled prayer, trusting what is holy—offers an intelli-
gible way to go when logic can't.

Jimmy Durante's old song about ambivalence suggests
what it's like to get caught in the crosshairs of an uncer-
tainty that must plague almost everyone at times. The first
line asked something like, "Did you ever get the feeling
that you wanted to stay, but then you also had the feeling
that you wanted to go?"

Double-mindedness has often left me twisting in the
wind like that. For instance, during the years I spent *wondering* how to live in these woods, before the day I actually moved, indecision hampered my decisionmaking.
Finally, my answer came—not in an audible voice, but as a
complete thought that nudged me into action: *Just get on
with it.* I realized the obvious—I'd never iron out all the
details beforehand. Right then and there I decided to follow the uncluttered advice of Proverbs 3:5–6:

> Trust in the Lord with all thine heart,
> And lean not unto thine own understanding.
>
> In all your ways acknowledge him, and He shall direct
> thy paths.

Forward movements of mind and heart precede all outer
progress. Goethe discovered that our commitment to do a
thing causes all manner of support to greet us along the
way. A hunch, a visual image from a film or dream, a
phone call from a pal fortifies us *after* we make up our

mind. That synchronicity helps me envision my goal as if it's already accomplished. Or hints at what to do. Higher consciousness—recollected thought; pure awareness—neutralizes indecision and its related anxieties.

We may notice only in hindsight that we've heard that "voice." As we launch a new career or reduce our credit-card debt, we see our edified mind in those concrete improvements. We get on a proper track *because* we've grasped the interior directive, because we're following it. Heeding that small, still voice is a contemplative's chief aim and occupation.

I am decidedly *not* saying that we're listening for audible "voices." We're not obeying sureal whispers to go shoot our great-aunt Hattie or some stressed-out bus driver for being rude. To Augustine Ichiro Okumura, the "most perfect prayer breathes in a heart that remains silent before God and knows how to listen to God."[1] In other words, hate and contempt have no place in prayer and are "totally contrary to prayer and cannot co-exist with it."[2] When distraught, a contemplative's only reliable medicine is praying in the Spirit.

In that unblemished communion, we keep still. We listen. We're not spouting a litany of empty words. We're actively engaged, *paying attention* to God's unbounded presence with us. Alas, we are ever-distracted, bombarded from every side by competing influences, and

> *because of our passions, pride, critical attitudes and prejudices we are unable to ponder and assimilate God's words contained within the daily events of our*

lives. . . . In the bargain, the sounds of our own "good" excuses intercept God's words like a strong shield, unknowingly making us deaf to God's message.[3]

Beware: mad hatters, cynics, and the depressed (anyone, in fact, whose rage, dysfunctions, or critical intellect rules the heart aggressively) should avoid listening to "voices." And stay away from overloads of *self*-directed, isolating solitude. The road to inner peace is not always peaceful. *Especially* when we're engulfed by turbulent emotions. It bears repeating: counseling may help us avoid shooting ourselves in the foot with crazed interiority. Not everyone requires counseling, however.

A law enforcement officer found that as family obligations grew, old friendships decreased. After getting married and having a baby, she separated from childhood friends who were single and "still into the dating scene." She had few intimates with whom to share her increasing interest in spiritual subjects, and followed an intuition to make new friends through classes at her church. Currently, despite her hectic working life and the demands of a young child, she "celebrates day-to-day victories" with like-minded friends. Here is someone who listens intelligently to the still, small voice within. She feels that her life "flows" because she's grounded in spiritual reality:

To some, it may look like I have it all: a loving husband, a wonderful child, an exciting career, a comfortable home, and direction in my life. All these things are just evidence of the consciousness I have cultivated. Some would just work for the evidence, or manifestations, without the solid foundation of that [spiritual] consciousness. That's when things fall apart or people have to constantly work to hold it together. I am grateful for all these gifts and use my gratitude to honor my family and my life as an expression of God.

Raimon Panikkar, an author, professor of religion, and scholar of contemplative intercultural dialogue, was originally ordained as a Catholic priest. He now "lives in the mountains of Catalunya trying to learn the wisdom of life."[4] When asked what form of meditation he recommends to novices who are comparing Zen, yoga, and other forms of contemplation, Panikkar simply outlined his own rigorous self-discovery principles:

I have given myself nine rules, or sutras:

1. Begin with myself (not trying to change others).
2. Begin within myself (hence, without impetus from outside).
3. Open myself to the whole of reality (not a "specialized" spirituality).
4. Begin where I myself am: no *tabula rasa,* no waiting for the best, ideal point of departure. For example, "once I have money . . . ," "once I get married . . . ," . . .
5. Do not consider the consequences. Here one needs a pure heart; otherwise one will be afraid. No one can calculate all consequences ahead of time, not even a com-

puter; and once I put my trust in a computer, I am no longer free.

6. Be in solidarity—hence, not in isolation. Solitude need not mean isolation; solidarity can mean group, family, friends, whatever.

7. Be self-motivated—hence, without outside help, without financial support from outside, without predetermination, without a fixed goal. The true self can never be motivated by a goal!

8. Be nonviolent—not straining the will, not wanting to overcome anything. Otherwise one is merely repressing constantly.

9. Always make a fresh start![5]

Stringency aside, Panikkar's notion of spiritual listening does *not* involve force. He's not straining his will. That rigidity thwarts contemplation. Methods and teachers that seem suitable for one person at a specific time and circumstance can be "disastrous" for others, and Panikkar reminds us to be wary of fixed formulas: "Pilgrim, there is no path; you yourself are making it by walking!"[6]

When we organize daily life to maximize contemplative experience, we may follow Panikkar's guideline and "begin with and with*in* ourselves." If we're typically obligated or involved with others they will invariably care what we do. We may do best by discerningly communicating with a few key constituents about our plans. To negotiate time off for a spiritual avocation from a college program or secretary's job requires a degree of collaborative planning. Our spouse, our management, or our doctoral committee will have a say. Here, too, each enhancement in *our* consciousness increases our ability to arrange mutually agreeable solutions. At minimum, we'll figure out what *we* need, having heard our transcendent directives above the din of everyone else's opinion.

If spiritual progress is our prime goal and mover, decisions related to ancillary matters can be perplexing. Logic argues against the unknown. We may imagine worst-case scenarios. We could picture friends or coworkers ridiculing us for getting active at our temple or church. We fear loneliness. Who will we talk to if we choose an unprecedented life? Praying for guidance is calming. It's also productive. As Thomas E. Clarke stresses, our prayers draw us "into a faith-response to life," and the soul is a "kind of center," "a divine dwelling" for witnessing and establishing right relationship with God and the universe: "Wherever there is a human being, then, there is a sphere of knowledge and power possessed of a certain infinitude, capable of intensively and extensively unlimited relationships with the whole of creation, and with the Creator, the divine center."[7]

Experiencing the givens of, say, a lengthy sabbatical or spiritual retreat, it's entirely possible that we'll want to adjust our course midstream. In the early spiritual walk wavering is normal, to be expected. Learning how not to waver is what our walk teaches us.

We're responding to the movement of the Spirit within. Sometimes that's a poetic influence—subtle, ineffable. At other times a wave of certainty washes over us. We're rightly focused. We hear "excellent things" (Proverbs 8:6) and gain an understanding heart. That heart often develops over time. One fortyish father of three told a group of us at dinner that he took a much-coveted sabbatical only to find himself frittering away his twelve months of unstructured days: "It took me an entire year to unwind—a whole precious year off—to learn how to use free time."

An educator wrote to say that only *after* joining a spiritual community did he begin to sense that it was a quasicult, intent on extracting huge financial and volunteer commitments from him. He felt trapped. He enjoyed the meditation program. He liked the people. But he felt cut off from freedom and his *own* wisdom. Should he stay or leave? His intuition seemed to say, "Return to your own religious roots." I never learned what he decided to do.

A centering prayer that invites our *hearing* in the Spirit lets us relax into our authentic directives. Scripture paves the way to that centering, *if* we pray more, listen more, and intellectualize less. Meditating on Scripture during *un*eventful times brings understanding. That is sure guidance when we're stressed—as in my middle-of-the-desert situation. Some divinely grounded verse invariably reveals our right course if we have saturated our thought processes with wisdom.

The reading of Scripture prunes us. A line here or there cuts to the quick of what we're about or need to do. Immersing ourselves in stillness, attending to selected, sacred texts of choice, we can become so intimate with God's thoughts that they become *our* thoughts. That is one way to discern the divinely inspired guidance that has been with us since before time.

Frequently my right course necessitates going against the grain of some feeling—fear or timidity, mostly. Nonetheless, those contrary choices have proved appropriate for me. A God-centered awareness is the organizing principle behind the certainty that "in the hidden parts [we] know wisdom" (Psalms 51:6).

Unwavering in Community

A self-made entrepreneur with many grown children and many more acres of prime real estate hoped to donate his land to a charitable foundation. For decades he had lived alone, building a somewhat reflective life and a large estate. He envisioned the compound being kept in trust, in perpetuity, for the public to enjoy. To ensure his family's wholehearted support, he talked things over with each offspring (and each respective spouse) before signing the legal documents. Today his vision can move forward because there were no surprises for the various stakeholders. For some of us to succeed, "selling all"—whether we move to a commune in Alaska or become a full-time hospice volunteer—could depend on our being totally open with loved ones. For others, privacy in all such matters is best.

A planning dialogue doesn't commit you to being joined at the hip with loved ones—especially if their habits or ideas are undermining. With certain family members, it's sometimes wiser to love from afar or to keep your plans to yourself. Only you know what's proper. More accurately, only you know if you rest in the commotion-less intelligence of the Spirit. You may give away a property or buy more, or start or end an enterprise, or relocate to Saigon. If the Spirit moves you, things tend to succeed—later, if not sooner.

Before quitting my tenured position, before selling my house, before relocating to the country, I took a measure of those closest to me to size up the effect of my relocation on them. Unlike the dictates of Panikkar's fifth sutra, I did consider consequences. That's probably one major distinction between casual and more austere contemplatives. I was moving lock, stock, and business to an obscure part of the state. I had contractual obligations, and did not want to be diverted by lack of support. I concocted a rough assessment tool to audit my readiness for various practical eventualities. For instance:

Finances	For the first year, how much cash flow, reserves, or insurance do I need? How much debt is too much?
Support links	What office supports are available in the new area? What's essential? What needed services can I obtain by mail, UPS or FedEx, computer, and phone?
Failure analysis	What are worst-case scenarios and a "Plan B" if best-laid plans fail?

A postulant who enters a religious order finds ready-made support. A monastery provides a constellation of concrete, valuable resources. Someone markets. Someone cooks. People take turns buying milk, tofu, and lettuce. There's usually a library and a laundry facility. A spiritual director comes around. Someone rings a bell when it's time to eat, sleep, or converse. Prayerful liturgies and holiday rituals are preestablished. Should anyone sprain an ankle or catch the flu, medical help is on tap. In other words, the affairs of daily living are pretty much handled so that all one's attention can be focused on God. That too can be a hefty weight. So *much* time to think.

Monastic practices can aggravate the inept or the double-minded. Meditation is demanding. It may seem simple—after all, one just sits in a chair, just observes the breath, or thoughts, or a line of prayer. However, objective observation also stirs ghosts. It brings back hurtful memories, the shame of cowardice, excesses, or addictions. Judgmental types are particularly vulnerable. If we're *too* logical, we obstruct spiritual growth. G. K. Chesterton's notion was that inordinate reason breeds insanity. It is the logician's head that splits:

> *Poets do not go mad; but chess-players do. Mathematicians go mad, and cashiers; but creative artists very seldom.*[8]

There's a noticeable downside to an aggressive intellect that can't tolerate spiritual mystery or entertain the lofty, perhaps ambiguous, vision of a healthy imagination. Long stretches of solitude can magnify a preexisting inclination to panic, to paranoia, to criticize minutiae—especially if intense rounds of prayer, meditation, or fasting are involved. Normal defense mechanisms intensify. Clearly each individual develops his or her spiritual sure-footings by living on the rock of a high, fine sanity.

Well-run, compassionate monasteries must routinely handle people's subjective turmoil. Postulants enter, struggle with cloistered living, and sometimes leave, sometimes beg to rejoin the order. The tormented may find it a victory to accept the fact that they're best suited to some other calling. All of us—gardeners, carpenters, philosophizing dreamers—desire wholesome growth, but if we're not micromanaging or morbidly analyzing each detail of spiritual experience, things go easier.

Independent casual contemplatives—the noncloistered breed—will create the infrastructures they need to support their revamped loyalties. They improvise. They take risks to create the worshipful life they love. We've seen that those who live in family settings must creatively guard chunks of time for worship. If they're not self-supporting, they are at least self-reliant. The contemplatives I know run bike repair shops or grain stores, or they're photographers or word processors, or they drive Federal Express vans. They may head up a Fortune 500–size company and be accountable to shareholders or a nitpicking management team, but they belong to themselves.

Good old horse-sense is an absolute must. Weird idiosyncrasies of diet or meditation can thwart a rightly ordered life. "Doing one's own thing"—a prune-juice and cabbage diet, the "anything goes" schedule of a slug—so easily accentuates the narcissism one seeks to lessen. When we pray in the Spirit, habitually relaxing into the superfluidity of pure consciousness, a kind of enlightened levelheadedness reigns. A maturing spirituality seeks tempered nourishment—neither boiling over with unruly passions nor freezing up from logic's rule. Properly hot. Properly cold. And tepid is completely useless, for as we read in Revelations 3:16, "because you are lukewarm, and neither hot nor cold, I will spit you out of My mouth."

Learning to be steady in the face of spiritual choices takes practice. At least for me, that new normalcy was novel. It took time and a bit of doing to be clear and outspoken, and appropriate, as situations require. A sure, faith-filled walk is nothing special, but it is a revised way of being.

Contemplatives Are Not "Special"

Everywhere in Scripture we find stories of ordinary people who lead holy lives. Despite doubts and pressure, their receptivity to God's Word is reliable. The poor widow who threw her last measly coin into the communal treasury box was called "blessed" by Jesus of Nazareth (Mark 12:44). She was in dire straits, but gave out of an unwavering faith. Once again, such stories teach us to relax into who we are, and to beware of scribes who love "salutations in the marketplaces, and the chief seats in the synagogues and the uppermost rooms at the feasts, [who] devour widows' houses and for a pretense make long prayers: these shall receive damnation" (Mark 12:38–40).

The anointed came from the unwashed throngs. Old, toothless women gave their last crumbs of bread to passing strangers, just because they realized that those travelers were prophets of God. These commonplace saints were graced with things and with *Truth*. They received precious oils and water to drink in times of drought and ate manna from heaven during widespread famine.

We read story after story of unspectacular fishermen and low-ranking soldiers devoted to virtue, to decency, to "things above and not below." Just as in our day: students, cab drivers, and rock stars alike hunger after life's deep truths. We all are famished for our own integrity, our breath of life—for God with us. That could partly explain our global admiration of the reflective arts—basket weaving, woodcarving, glassblowing—all those crafts done in meditative absorption, so mindfully that the attention of both artist and appreciator gets redirected toward eternity. We know how those pursuits restore and fulfill us.

One Saturday at dawn we start pruning a pink vine-rose. Time evaporates. Presently it's noon, but we forget to eat the tuna sandwich waiting for us in the fridge. Ignoring the grumblings of our stomach we command our knees to bend. Still busy at dusk, we're now imagining how to prune back our excesses, "hearing" that small still voice that says, "Trim your own affairs so that you'll blossom luxuriantly like this budding vine-rose, for ... 'every branch that beareth fruit, he purgeth it, that it may bring forth more fruit'" (John 15:2).

A casually contemplative life is not haphazard, not totally "casual." It is fully committed to worship and therefore not like an occasional, tranquilizing hobby.

Devotion, gratitude, the sense of oneness with eternity—these are substantive perceptual motifs, the very filter through which we see, feel, think. The life itself integrates all outer forms of prayer with a seeing, hearing heart. Whether our days are mundane or regal, churched or unchurched, we can live a prayer of awakening as we appreciate the sanctity of creation. Life itself can be simultaneously unspectacular and rich with praise and prayer. We are born to comprehend that paradox *if* we burn to live our purity of heart—that is to say, if we demonstrate our heart's consuming Fire within the active givens of each ordinary day. God's Word assures us that the sincere of heart, however mundane their life, can reenter the Garden. Like a priest friend of mine who's been ill for two years and oddly blessed by it, we may find that our life isn't pretty or easy, but that it feels like a lovely organizing prayer, as it did for the venerable country parson and poet George Herbert:

> These are thy wonders. Lord of love,
> To make us see we are but flowers that glide,
> Which where we once can find and prove,
> Thou hast a garden for us, where to bide.[9]

IDEAS FOR THE SPIRITUAL WALK

Scheduling Time for Contemplation

In *The Mentor's Spirit,* I explained how I restructured progressive amounts of time for spiritual reflection. I began slowly. Honored old contractual obligations, but altered new ones. Set aside one day (Sunday) for doing nothing. Learned to say yes and no clearly, so that family and close friends didn't encroach on the hours I'd scheduled for reading, studying, or just puttering. I took spiritual breaks—from several weeks to a year's sabbatical—and attended spiritual retreats and month-long meditation programs. Of course, I studied at home. I took my first year off (without pay) in the late seventies and have taken yearlong moratoriums every five years or so since then.

Reading that disclosure, one interviewer berated me. She said that parents with young children or people who depend on a full-time job can't afford the luxury of taking a year off. I agreed. A lengthy cessation of work is not an entitlement. Having been self-supporting since my teens, I'd *earned* time off. Someone else might plan and save for a BMW or a summer in Paris.

We have discussed the desirability of protecting at least one period a day for contemplative prayer and spiritual study. Consider expanding on that. With calendar in hand, with significant others in mind, ponder the pleasure—and wisdom—of scheduling first short, then longer, spiritual moratoriums. When, for instance, might you take . . .

- One night off each week
- One day off each month
- One long weekend a quarter
- One week a year for spiritual renewal, perhaps at a church, synagogue, or spiritual retreat

- Two to three weeks off (or more) every year (or alternative year) for a nonstructured, contemplative break
- One long sabbatical (from several months to a year) every five to seven years for advanced study, retreats, travel, gardening—whatever.

If we prearrange conditions—much as we allocate funds and days off for a vacation—we're more likely to integrate a spiritual practice and a sabbatical into our workaday life.

Don't forget that most cloistered monks *work*. It's true, their chief task is to learn to love—in freedom. Yet monks are also supported by what they do *within* the monastery's setup. Time off within that formal arrangement may be scarce. Our lives in the world of family and business offer enviable flexibilities to experience a divine affluence.

6

Life as Wholesome Prayer

For with thee is the fountain of life:
In thy light shall we see light.

—Psalms 36:9

Thirty years ago, Leslie R. Smith compared humans to a pigeon that had been caged since birth. When its owner decided to set the bird free, he tossed it into the air and watched it fly away with ease. The only problem was that the pitiful creature didn't know how to *stop*. It crashed to earth on its little feathered head and died.

Looking around his world, Smith noticed plenty of self-starters but few self-stoppers. He asked, *Do we really know how to stop flying about?* Today his question has added relevance. In the last three decades matters on the home front have worsened. Our schedules are frenetic. Like Smith's self-starters, we are often victimized by our own calendars:

> *Even seventh and eighth graders now need appointment books in order to keep their activities in mind. We often (or usually) drop into bed at night so exhausted that we are too tired to pray, even though that was our intention; we are too tired to sleep and when we finally drift off, our slumber is fitful and we wake up more tired than when we went to bed.*[1]

I know a few wholesome self-stoppers. They're conscious—aware of what they want to do with time. They know when to say, "Enough is enough." They shut off their computers so that they can read, listen to *A Prairie Home Companion,* or tinker with toy trains. They unclog a choked-up itinerary so that they can play with their child. They take naps. They sleep soundly at night (unlike the two-thirds of us who complain of sleep disorders). They enjoy vacations. They are the self-definers who *trust* what they need or value and feel challenged—not overwhelmed—by the prospect of *being more*. For some, the phrase "being more" means doing less.

"Being more" flows from pure awareness. We meet ourselves in a wordless peace despite the lively context of our usual day. That peace accompanies us wherever we go, lets us accept ourselves where we are now, as we are, not only during times of formal stillness but also in informal situations—at our desks, waiting on line at the bank, browsing around the supermarket squeezing cantaloupes for ripeness. The purity that we experience while gazing out from the peak of Mount Everest or sitting in the lotus position in our den must at some point sweep *us* clean. The fruit of the Spirit—love, joy, peace, gentleness, forgiveness—arrives every which way, with ritual and without ritual, and when we least expect it, for "against such there is no law" (Galatians 5:23).

Praying in the Spirit curbs spirit*less* activity. This is decidedly *not* what has been called a "cheap solution"— that is, indiscriminately calling every activity prayer. I mean that after a period of contemplative prayer we encounter the juice—the force, the actual power—of the Holy Spirit *in us*. As we pray formally or sing hymns or sit in dainty, prayerful stillness, and *also* as we deal with the grubby givens of each typical day, we apprehend a luminosity as the phenomena around us. This is not an intellectual exercise. Not simply cerebral. It is experiential: we are aware of *light,* beams of love. We are grateful. We are praying.

Nourishment for that experience comes from formal spiritual practices, but also from, say, feelings and anxious, untenable choices that set our teeth on edge. In the seventies, Ram Dass aptly called this "grist for the mill." We needn't go anywhere explicitly "holy" to grow spiritually. Whatever's occurring right now is essential to our progress:

> *When someone gets you furious you know that the only reason you got angry is because you have a secret stashed model of how you think it ought to be,*

that you're holding on to. You realize that the person that got you angry is a teaching and in your mind you thank him. You get so eager to root out the stuff in you that's keeping you from getting on, from awakening, that you start to look for situations to force you to do it.[2]

A theologian might frame the matter differently. For instance, Augustine Ichiro Okumura writes:

There is nothing, not even sin itself—negligence, anger, hatred—that cannot become prayer. . . . In these moments think of the pearl oyster: . . . In due time a magnificent pearl is made from the grain of sand. In like manner the animosities and antipathies that make their way into our hearts are seemingly indigestible pebbles. However, if we keep them wrapped, as it were, in our prayer, they will become pearls of love.[3]

It's not comfortable to keep a coworker who's rejected us "wrapped in prayer." But as a friend confided, "That's what living for God means—we practice loving our neighbor as ourselves. We want others to forgive us, so reconciliation is our job too." Everyday situations can draw us *informally* into a mind of such total engagement that we enter the narrow, paradoxical way that leads to greater life. We fail a thousand times. Failing is irrelevant—it's not our concern here. Faithfulness to a high, fine standard is what we're after. So we must ask ourselves, "What's my relationship with God? Have I been listening to God or have I closed my heart?" If we're practicing the spiritual walk, eventually we'll encounter the power—and the peace—of the Spirit. We'll just keep working at it—without an eye on our perfections or lack thereof—and eventually grace comes. Grace is unmerited. We don't and can't earn it.

We know we're praying "in the Spirit" *if* we:

- forget ourselves while attending to the sacred Transcendent, beyond ourselves;
- progressively turn our attention to the things of God in daily activity; and
- increasingly reflect the *fruits* of the Spirit—patience, love, mercy—in our lives.

We're not to be enchanted with our own "light"—*our* special powers, *our* achievements, *our* compassionate nature. We're serving Life itself spontaneously, not egotistically, not legalistically, "not in the oldness of the letter of the Law" (Romans 7:6). Both formal and informal prayer cultivate that dynamic spontaneity, and for the balance of this chapter we'll explore selected features of *informal* prayer.

Living from the Inside Out

Often on TV shows experts on spirituality claim that forgiveness comes primarily by force. In essence they say,

"Forgiveness is not automatic. It's so very difficult, you must coerce yourself each day to forgive others." I'm inclined to prefer Saint Bonaventure's advice: to live joyfully, with sweetness and a tender forgiving heart, we'll simply become individuals of prayer.

In particular, contemplative prayer roots out fear and rage, eventually replacing these emotions with the gentle unction and grace of the Holy Spirit. That teaches us *all* things—including forgiveness.[4]

Those experts are right about one thing: forgiveness *is* unnatural. However, praying in the Spirit is natural. It alone plugs us into *super*natural ability and a reprieving heart. Forgiveness is no intellectual abstraction.

Here's another way of looking at it. An audience member at a bookstore reading in Guerneville, California, told our group the following related story:

My husband is a law enforcement officer. He's a very refined, contemplative man. Each day after work, no sooner does he enter the house than he goes into his study to pray and meditate. The family knows not to speak to him until he's had that quiet time. My stepson will tell you: my husband is a peaceful man, despite the brutality that he sees daily. Prayer is his reconciler.

The general public would be surprised to know how many police officers pray—how thoughtful and spiritual they've got to be to do their jobs without going mad. We hear of police violence against citizens. Real prayer could remedy that.

True prayer heals. It transforms and reconciles *us*. Softens our heart. Spontaneously swayed by the peace we encounter while praying in the Spirit, we let go of old slights. Over time our memory bank is cleansed of ancient bruises. Even when we don't "feel" anything in contemplative prayer, something good is happening.

We may never completely *forget* the death of a child, a spouse's betrayal, or a parent's abandonment of us in childhood. We may be unwilling to sit calmly in the same room with old tormentors, but we do forgive. Forgiveness is already *with* us. It's eternal—like love. Our job is to remember that, and to return experientially to the forgiven and the forgiving state. At some point our slate of consciousness is washed clean.

Contemplative prayer is delicately nuanced, and not so much concerned with bodily posture as with attitude of heart. Without some sense of the power and pathos of the indwelling Spirit, I seriously question anyone's ability to forgive, or to achieve psychological health, or even to heal. Moreover, we don't know in advance what means the Holy Spirit will use to comfort us.

In an interview, ethnobotanist Kathleen Harrison explained how she came to view even *interspecies* communion as prayer: "Talking to the essences of species other than human and asking them to be present and to intervene to heal us or to grow, or thanking them for being so beautiful—all of these are a kind of prayer."[5]

Harrison believes we can call on what's wild for help and can commune intimately with plants, butterflies, or bees for new, unexpected healings. She describes one woman with advanced ovarian cancer whose Buddhist healer had no "in-depth relationship to plants" but who intuited the significance of the woman's magnificent garden. Sitting by the woman's bed, the healer invoked the presence of all the plants. She paid proper attention to them and invited them in to be present as companions in the healing.[6]

For many, such tales of healers talking to plants or using them as healing agents is a huge stretch. Although the Bible tells us that the Lord gave us every plant-yielding seed on the surface of the earth to be food (Genesis 1:29) many prefer their chemo straight up and thank you very much. Ah, but spiritualities *differ.* Harrison reports that the woman with ovarian cancer is now in remission. So please, to each her own.

The proof is in the pudding: prayer heals. And prayer differs. And prayer graces us, without force, drawing us deep into the subtlest, silent realms of the subtle. Let us remain there—as long and self-forgetfully as possible, even into our busy day.

If we can just transcend our usual, clunky thought processes during, say, a weekend of weeding or cross-country skiing, we can amplify our grasp of what praying in the Spirit is for us. Then when we retire to a barn-studio to sculpt in solitary fashion, we can recall that state and use our art to move beyond self—to concentrate so seamlessly on what we're doing that we exit our problematic world of worry or stiffening joints to experience what one person called "frictionless focus."

Prayer, reflective journal exercises, even work and relationships can be so filled with the Spirit that we become saturated with awe, with gratitude. We feel blessed to be alive. Despite pain, loss, or frustration, we then sigh in thanksgiving along with the psalmist,

Thou hast anointed my head with oil;
My cup overflows,
Surely goodness and mercy will follow me all the days of
   my life,
And I will dwell in the house of the Lord forever.

                                 —Psalms 23: 5–6

Don't get me wrong: praying formally may well involve ritual, corporate worship, liturgy, hymns—all the sacred elements of our respective creeds. Yet intimate communion is possible only when we're with and *in* the Spirit. With eyes either open or shut, kneeling or sitting, we can see beyond the visible world and perceive that inordinate, self-existent power is our Life. Saint Augustine, speaking to God, said in effect: You were always with me; *it was I who was not always with You.*

Our normal distractedness makes it seem that the Holy Spirit is absent. It is we who are missing. Contemplatives long to be fully present with God. They arrange space in their lives for the Spirit, making room in their thoughts, their schedules, their habits and hearts for that "food of grown men" that is converted into the Spirit.[7]

To set a finite, prescribed time for devotion is all well and good. It is important. (I've already said that for contemplatives a morning worship is a must.) Contemplatives want much more and therefore don't devalue the *rest* of their day. Rather, they come at things so as to give themselves over to their spiritual call. That means surrendering to vocation like any professional.

Born surgeons sacrifice their own health for the well-being of others. They endure long, intense work cycles, go without sleep, relinquish time off, and may even risk dissension at home out of devotion to their patients. Born parents sacrifice their careers for the twenty-four-hour care of their children. Picasso's admission that he sacrificed everything to his art—a peaceful family life, friendships, even himself— captures this principle. Such renunciations are not born of workaholism. To work slavishly out of fear or suppressed rage is dysfunction. To labor from love is to enter the "strait gate" of vocation that, practiced rightly, unites with the life of Spirit in our life.[8]

Should we choose to follow a "no holds barred" vocation, we still do our grunt work—but mindfully. We feel strengthened to tackle some—not all—of the things we don't like. We still take business trips when we'd rather stay home. Suffer fools as best we can. Scrub toilets till they sparkle. Clean storm windows. Honor the nitpicky rules of the IRS. Sometimes these obligations drop in on us, as if from above. The unity we seek, the wholeness or *telio* we crave, probably comes from meeting these demands.

When a young friend and her husband became parents of triplets, their responsibilities increased tenfold. They both work outside of the home, so their energy drains were nearly total. Their first duty was to parenting—not ministering to their fatigue. The saying "You do what you've got to do" explains their situation.

Another youthful newlywed couple found themselves saddled with formidable travel schedules related to their management jobs. The modern pair chose to advance professionally. Mutual ambition nourished their marriage. Even when they lacked time for each other, they were together—working toward common goals and a shared vision of their future. Although at the time they'd have preferred a more relaxed, reflective life, today they're glad they chose as they did. I don't know how parents of triplets or bicoastal career couples practice contemplative disciplines. It's possible that a ten-minute morning or before-sleep meditation suffices for a few years. It may help to remember that the habitual practice of meeting one's commitments *is* also prayer.

If we approach our responsibilities as if we're living for that infinite, unseen Good beyond ourselves, we'll bolster our contemplative mind. That's because it takes a steady, sincere focus to tackle our distinctive grunt work in a recollected way. However, that's no guarantee of popularity.

My contemplative tendencies have left me with a short attention span for coffee-klatch chitchat or cocktail party socializing. Once, during a neighbor's Sunday bash, I was taken with the balmy night. Soft, warm air lured me out of the stuffy living room to the patio. Enveloped in an enjoyable reverie, I soon drifted out of my neighbor's yard and inadvertently ambled back home—two blocks away—without so much as a good-bye or a thank-you. I was never invited back.

Probably to console myself, I've reflected since then on an instructive anecdote that G. K. Chesterton tells about Saint Thomas Aquinas. When he was still an obedient Dominican friar, Aquinas was advised by his superiors to attend a banquet at the royal court of King Louis IX of France. "Rather sulkily," Aquinas went to the party. His hosts steered his "reluctant bulk to a seat in the royal banquet hall," where Aquinas—while courteous to everyone—spoke hardly at all, given as he was to a "permanent trance of reflection." For a while he was quite forgotten "in the most brilliant and noisy clatter in the world: the noise of French talking." He suddenly shocked the court, by striking his portly fist like a club on the table and then, "like a man in a grip of a dream," by crying out something that had little to do with the babble at hand.[9] Chesterton's graphic portrayal of that scene provides an insight into the nature of contemplative preoccupation:

> It was something that might alternatively be called his moral attitude, or his temperamental predisposition, or the purpose of his life so far as social and human effects were concerned: for he knew better than most of us that there is but one purpose in this life and it is one that is beyond this life.[10]

Not without good reason do contemplatives decline certain social engagements.

Our new mandate to love others as ourselves encompasses a mature compassion, but that does not automatically imply conventional fellowship. And therein lies the rub: putting love of God first is not a social task. Nor is that love always attractive. It's downright incomprehensible.

We can expect loyalties to shift. Ours and those of others. Put plainly, we're crossing over a conventional threshold of experience, moving toward intimate Oneness with God. This is cumulative. Each time we pray in the Spirit, we're adding to the directives already received from within, building a relationship, reversing a deadly system of programmed allegiances. That experience transforms us at our ground of being.

This transformation introduces another paradox: we may be leaving *special,* exclusive relationships while concurrently living for humanity at large. Spiritual maturity embraces what Raimon Panikkar calls the "entire *karmic* net with its foundations, the entire reality."[11] Our oneness with others is impersonal. Quoting the *Rig Veda,* he proposes that in a spirit of oneness we now stretch "to the farthest corners of the world."[12]

It is ironic that to serve a network of others in that spirit of oneness we stop being *humanly* consumed. Dietrich Bonhoeffer explored this eloquently. He was a social creature, a gifted leader, a veritable saint who died at the hands of the Gestapo, executed by special order of Heinrich Himmler. Bonhoeffer was also deeply contemplative. He knew, as few others do, how corrosive to spiritual well-being *human* enchantments can be. In the journal he kept while imprisoned in concentration camp, he wrote that we must never become so overtaken by any-one else's charisma that we fall under their spell.

Bonhoeffer stressed the inherent dangers of human communities where "the humanly strong person" is "in his element, securing for himself the admiration, the love, or the fear of the weak. Here human ties, suggestions, and bonds are everything."[13]

Lacking a wholesome *spiritual* foundation, even best-friend and marriage relationships can get distorted. One person could hold power and influence over another who repeatedly submits, appeases, clings. This is the antithesis of spiritual health.

Bonhoeffer writes that God originally intended our life to be "mediated through the indwelling Spirit." When we bow down to *persons,* we warp our existence, and pervert ourselves. In those circumstances, even if we experience some religious change of heart, that too debases us, for our conversion is "effected, not by the Holy Spirit, but by a man, and therefore has no stability."[14]

With characteristic bluntness, Thomas Merton told aspiring contemplatives something similar: *Grow up.* If we're summoned to live contemplatively, we must face that fact and stop being "unduly influenced by the slogans of people who don't know our problems." To Merton, that growing up, that facing of facts, demands that we refuse to be involved in "useless, foolish substitutes" for the contemplative life we want, and resist all encroach-ments or threats to our contemplative life (not to mention its disciplines), and relinquish a "dead, formalistic set of pseudocontemplative routines."[15]

His three simple edicts reinforce the hard sayings of Jesus of Nazareth: to know God, we must leave mother, father, and friend behind; must love God above all, *and* love our neighbor as ourselves.

The Psychological Backbone

The fainthearted and the people pleasers have much work to do to satisfy the tough love of a typical contemplative's day. Unequivocally, anyone called to live prayerfully needs to say yes and no clearly; adroitly, but without apology: Nonambiguity serves contemplative life.

On the other hand, to glamorize solitude and monastic living, especially when we're wrongly motivated, is, in the long run, to invite existential dread. We may mistakenly believe that a contemplative existence is what we want when we merely feel overwhelmed. One bright executive says he scours travel brochures when he's fatigued: "I just want to escape the pressure. I don't take my wish to run away too seriously. After a weekend spent with some quality couch-potato time and the sports channel, I forget about quitting my job."

Some may say, "Well, this doesn't sound particularly healthy," but even computers get down time. A day spent napping, and so-called useless tasks can benefit self-renewal.

If we embark on a contemplative journey hoping to magnify ourselves by means of what we fancy is an exclusivity of lifestyle, we'll also exacerbate our troubles. For example, some people call every difficulty their "dark night." That's not only presumptuous, it's also counter-productive. We're kidding ourselves, and manufacturing problems when we dramatize the slightest snag in medita-tion. A degree of restlessness in any discipline is to be expected. The inability to sit still or find instant comfort in prayer goes with the territory.

Merton stressed repeatedly that most of us are imma-ture—not grown-up enough spiritually to experience either a dark night or an authentic religious crisis. Our imagined "emptiness" is usually a narcissism stuffed to the brim with pride:

> *An emptiness that is deliberately cultivated, for the sake of fulfilling a personal spiritual ambition, is not empty at all: it is full of itself. It is so full that the light of God cannot get into it anywhere; there is not a crack or a corner left where anything else can wedge itself into this hard core of self-aspiration which is our option to live centered in our own self. Such "emptiness" is in fact the emptiness of hell . . . consequently anyone who aspires to become a con-templative should think twice before he sets out on the road.*[16]

There is a strong psychological component or backbone to spiritual growth. Its markers are attainable. First, though, we may need to get a little assertive. That's a basic life skill and we'll return to this topic in the next chapter. Interpersonal distresses can arise when we choose to spend blocks of time alone or when we refuse to accommodate the telephone ramblings or party plans of old chums. Even if we're not traditionally religious, not church- or temple-goers, a contemplative life requires inner fortitude. In the normal workings of our human community it takes guts to say what you're about.

IDEAS FOR THE SPIRITUAL WALK

Contemplating True Joy

After choosing a time and place where you will be undisturbed, sit in stillness for a few minutes. Let your mind settle down, your breathing become even and "soft." Consider mulling over the following lines, or select a verse you prefer, for yet another few minutes:

> This day is holy unto our Lord;
> Neither be ye sorry; for the joy of the Lord is your
> strength.
>
> —Nehemiah 8:10

Describe your experience of simple sitting.

7

An Infinite Progression

The eternal God is thy refuge,
And underneath are the everlasting arms . . .

—Deuteronomy 33:27

Binx Bolling, the eccentric stockbroker in Walker Percy's poetic novel *The Moviegoer*, confesses that he's felt more sadness than joy when he's with old pals. Having observed a gloss of sociability covering true closeness, Binx says good-bye. He wishes them well, but moves on. His friends can't believe he doesn't want to hang out anymore. Binx is fun. He's no prig. They continue to drop by his place in Gentilly, New Orleans, inviting him to the Quarter to tour bars, listen to music, visit the whores. Binx declines. Again he wishes them well, but he can't muster enthusiasm to join them on these outings:

As for me, I stay home . . . and turn on TV. Not that I like TV so much, but it doesn't distract me from the wonder. That is why I can't go to the trouble they go to. It is distracting, and not for five minutes will I be distracted from the wonder.[1]

Binx knows what he needs and speaks up for it. He's a contemplative guy, in love with "the wonder" in his own way. I'd guess that Julian of Norwich and John Muir, if they were around, and probably Saint Francis and my various phoneless and meditating friends would empathize with Binx. I sure do.

Once, John Muir wrote to a friend that if people only knew how glad he was to be alone in the wilderness they'd never again invite him to join them in society. He said he was learning to live close to his friends without ever seeing them. Only another contemplative could relate to this, and even some monastics cannot.

James Laughlin, publisher of many of Thomas Merton's books, wrote that before Merton lived in his hermitage in the woods he groused that there was too much diverting conversation in the monastery:

We think that Trappist monks don't talk, but that isn't necessarily so. They may talk as much as they want with their hands, in sign language. This irritated Tom and may have been a reason why he longed for the life of a hermit. . . . I found a curious contradiction there, that this man who loved people and was in touch with so many of them all over the world wanted to isolate himself.[2]

True contemplatives get it. They're not isolated. "Isolation" is an inaccurate term. That's *not* what's going on. So fundamental is this tension between love of solitary life and duty to other normal activity that Saint Gregory, who guided both cloistered monks and busy pastors, taught that contemplative and active living were in opposition. To break through most deeply into the mystery of God, he said, we must "rest from exterior action and cleave *only* to the desire of the Maker."[3] Merton helpfully reminds us that any earthly vocation necessarily combines both activity and prayer. It's just a matter of degree.[4]

Whatever we think of a man like Binx, a casually contemplative life can reconcile the conflict we feel between activity and interiority. As has been said, there is no "outside" to the infinite. That sense shapes some rightly ordered balance with which we meet individual obligations and also worship. Parents of young children, corporate negotiators, and chefs at the Four Seasons could possess strong contemplative drives. Each one who is engaged in a material world must find ways to merge duty and reflection, since

> *the answer is not liturgy alone, or meditation alone, but a full and many-sided life of prayer in which all these things can receive their proper emphasis. This emphasis will tend to differ in different persons, and in different individual vocations. . . .*

> *If necessary, obstacles must be removed and discreet adjustments can and should be made, so that the*

*monastic community will produce a flowering of
every spirit and every type of prayer.*

*What is said here for monks applies also, with cer-
tain adjustments, to all the faithful.[5]*

It often feels as if our more extroverted friends—the
"active livers"—aggravate our conflict. In fact, if we're
truly summoned to a contemplative life, it's our business
to restore equilibrium to every aspect of life. So-called
problems clarify our purposes. These are a disguised blessing. Some things will *have* to go. Balance requires the
development of what John Briggs calls "choosing-and-
arranging skill."[6] Briggs is speaking generally about artis-
tic genius, and sums up choosing-arranging skill with
Virginia Woolf's words: the artist's "chief task is to find a
hidden reality and communicate it to her reader."[7] That's
our task as well.

Not only artists and writers, but mothers, fathers, and
postal workers long to express their sacred realities. Who
doesn't want to communicate their intuitive, spiritual
sense of being? Without such expressions, we live only
half a life—distracted and inharmonious—no matter how
much wealth or bedazzling achievements we garner.
Nowhere is that spiritual bankruptcy more poignant than
in the addicted, the mentally ill or chronically depressed.

The nightly news recently reported the suicide of a
youthful, rising Hollywood star. Plagued with manic
depression, unable to shake a long-standing drug habit,
the young man apparently shocked family and friends by

hanging himself in a cheesy motel. When one of his costars was interviewed about his death, the reporter asked, "How do you explain your friend's suicide? He had everything to live for—good looks, a successful career, wealth and fame, loyal friends, a loving, supportive family." The glamorous woman, sounding more sage than star, replied, "Yes, he had everything *except* that essential quiet on the inside that makes life worth living."

A contemplative mind-set gives us that "essential quiet on the inside." The fruits of its disciplines ultimately permeate our thoughts with spiritual intelligence—wisdom, intuitive knowing, inspired thinking.[8] Without that "essential quiet on the inside" our tangible assets can feel worthless. Yet even with, say, a meager pension or poor health, that essential quiet blesses us. For instance, Marshall Stewart Ball, a youngster who can neither speak nor walk, seems infused with deep spiritual stillness. He draws wisdom from that silence—for himself and for others. Now in his teens, Ball has been writing since he was six years old as a way of sharing his philosophy of divine love with others. Despite, perhaps because of, the silence in which he lives, he seems to have become a voice of spiritual wisdom.[9]

Harmony means accord. In stillness of a spiritual sort we find the comfort that includes composure, serenity, and peace of mind. It is endlessly gratifying, endlessly organizing.

Almost everyone longs for the wherewithal to live harmoniously. Yet no one experiences spiritual comfort without learning how to listen inwardly, or actualize what theologian Karl Rahner called an encounter with silence.

That encounter touches "the depths of [our] being where [we] are most truly 'I.'"[10] It also prompts us to say, "Enough is enough," to some vexing activities and people.

To extricate ourselves from unproductive pastimes we need finesse, even a degree of firmness. We may need to teach ourselves not to feel falsely guilty about disappointing those who, as Merton notes, have no heart or feeling for what we value. Merton himself was extraordinarily productive, often working on several projects at a time. He saw both active and contemplative pursuits as part of life, commenting that Mary and Martha are, after all, sisters.[11] How much weight we give to each aspect of our life is up to us.

I have suggested several ways to choose-and-arrange the comforts of a casually contemplative life while meeting normal commitments. Even while living in a material world we can learn to *be* of the spiritual by:

- shouldering the "beams of love"
- developing a hearing ear and a seeing eye
- reflecting the divine Oneness distinctively
- untangling our affairs
- not wavering in our loyalty to our values
- praying in the Spirit daily

Emotional Maturity

A word more about "growing up" spiritually: emotional maturity is the bedrock on which contemplative habits are built. You can't protect your time in the morning for daily prayer and meditation, or study further on these themes at night, or use your three-day weekend for a spiritual retreat, if you can't tell your loved ones what you need.

"Going along to get along" is *not* spiritual. It's exhausting and distracting. Passive and unhealthy. No matter how regularly we attend a place of worship, sit down to formal prayer, recite our favorite Psalm, if we can't think or speak up for ourselves, we won't assert our spiritual best. The unassertive can't protect their lives from intrusion. They sorely limit their growth. Further, the inordinately reasonable are too often masochistically compliant—"slaves in the spiritual order." For example, men who endure endless encroachments probably won't say yes to the fishing vacation or the men's outing they want and deserve. Women who endure endless encroachments probably won't say yes to the health spa weekend or the women's retreat they want and deserve.

Rather than confront the inept, the hurtful, or the time wasters in our midst, many of us choose to suffer. Rather than feel uncomfortable while we're strengthening our muscles of verbal adequacy (for example, practicing assertiveness skills or appropriate aggression), we sweep our frustrations under the rug of accommodation.

If you identify with such self-brutalizing "reasonableness," then before setting sail for a contemplative lifestyle, it may help to train yourself to speak up for what you need, want, and deserve.

Psychiatrist Natalie Shainess writes that healthy autonomy is "freedom from tyranny, *outer or inner,* freedom from the tyranny of exclusion or mistreatment; freedom from compulsion."[12] Wholesome autonomy is linked to a courageous, truthful communication style. It is also appropriately restrained. Openness has its limits, as Shainess tells the ultracompliant:

> *Urge yourself to express yourself directly, unequivocally, even if you are afraid of the response. Resolve that if you are uncertain of the worth of what you are about to say, you will at least keep your mouth shut and say nothing. . . .*
>
> *There is simply no doubt that it is always preferable to keep your silence rather than volunteering something that may be hurtful to you. . . . Try not to concern yourself with what the other person is thinking. Concentrate instead on what it is you want to say and wait until your statement is clear before you make it. . . . You will be, in effect, training yourself to exercise a new style.*[13]

Growing up spiritually means moving beyond lifeless roles and dead rituals. A spiritually maturing individual is no phony and often speaks bluntly. We must either correct or let go of relationships that undermine our life or somehow don't work, learning to say what's what as honestly and kindly as we can. Speaking the truth also calls for staying present. We're paying *attention* to whatever is happening—in a situation, in others, in ourselves. That's inward listening, inward watching. And little things count.

A joke or remark that's even fractionally degrading to

us can be deftly turned to our advantage, simply by refusing to agree or telling our companions, "I'd never say that about myself." The inward stirring, that small still voice—the scratching inside—can guide us. *If* we pay attention. Practice is in order.

Some other application exercises for that practice follow. Again, these are for your evaluation. Each of us must tailor such ideas to an appropriate life-context, to our values, temperament, emotional readiness, and personal specifications. Let us not shoot ourselves in the foot for lack of good sense.

Starting the Day

Time can be your own, much as Bicknell Young, a Christian Scientist writing in the early 1900s, might have meant when he wrote:

> *Know that the false belief of time has no dominion over you—you have dominion over it! . . . When you awaken, know that you have the time and opportunity to do all things that you need to do this day. . . . Again declare [that there is only one God in Whom] all things are accomplished. If you stick to this, you will have plenty of time and opportunity to take care of each task before you.*[14]

As soon as you wake up in the morning, *before opening your eyes,* and certainly before jumping out of bed to start your riotous routines, reflect on Young's words. Consider affirming silently, "There is only one God, or self-existent Life, in Whom all things are accomplished. Because the Spirit guides me, I now always have time to do all that must be done in a calm and orderly manner."

Further Study

Consider forming a study group of like-minded, contemplatively inspired associates. Your purpose is to read about, and support one another's, wholesome autonomy. Depending on its makeup, a study group can be a profound setting in which to explore various methods of meditation, like observational versus mantra methods. If you can't find an appropriate group, and if you're qualified, consider starting an adult education course. Or, do as the four long-distance friends did in chapter 2: locate trusted others with whom to teleconference. An extensive bibliography (listing some of my favorite books) follows this chapter. It includes dozens of books that you can find at any library. Each one offers ideas for further study. Your pastor, rabbi, or spiritual director can suggest other approaches to study or may even want to facilitate a discussion group occasionally. Whether you meet weekly, monthly, or even quarterly, decide how you want to organize your discipline of study. Nothing is worse than an aimless, unfocused discussion group supposedly gathered to plumb the depths of some theme, but rambling without purpose.

Study as a Contemplative Discipline

In his helpful book *Celebration of Discipline,* Richard Foster outlines various spiritual disciplines. He calls them inner, outer, and corporate disciplines. Among these is one he calls "the discipline of study." What a great notion. As meditation on Scripture is mentioned throughout these pages, why not assess the possibilities of gathering a small group to read and discuss Scripture or agree-upon sacred texts or books on the contemplative life? Imagine the dialogue.

The chief aim of a *discipline* of study is to see into "the reality of a given situation, encounter, [or] book." In this case, the reality we want to see into is the contemplative life and the formation of spiritual maturity. Foster lists four elements of a discipline of study:

1. *Repetition:* Channeling the mind regularly and in a specific direction—as in a training affirmation or to ingrain a habit of thought.
2. *Concentration:* Focusing the attention and reaching new levels of understanding.
3. *Reflection*: Seeing things from a new, divine, perspective.
4. *Humility:* Approaching our study correctly—that is, as students, not as teachers: "Arrogance and a teachable spirit are mutually exclusive."[15]

Foster also suggests three rules that might nicely structure each conversation:

- *Understanding:* What has the author said?
- *Interpretation:* What does the author really mean?
- *Evaluation:* In my opinion, is the author correct?[16]

I offer a fourth guideline, namely:

- *Application:* What is my "take-away" from this reading? How, responsibly and explicitly, might I apply some idea to add value, wisdom, or effectiveness to my own contemplative life?

To learn more about contemplative life, concentrate primarily on books written *by* contemplatives—individuals who have lived or are living simply and reflectively—rather than books written by those merely offering their academic theories *about* the subject. Memoirs by (and biographies of) artists, writers, poets, and inventors can be marvelous companions in that study. All such creative contributors must tap into an unseen, creative reality to accomplish their vision in the real world.

Forgiveness

No spiritual life progresses fruitfully without developing forgiveness: the pardon, absolution, or overlooking of hurt. Francis of Paola is reported to have said,

> *Pardon one another so that later on you will not remember the injury. The recollection of an injury is in itself wrong. It adds to our anger, nurtures our sin*

*and hates what is good. It is a rusty arrow and poi-
son for the soul. It puts all virtue to flight.*[17]

We would do well to practice forgiveness every day. As
mentioned, we need not strain. If you incorporate a forgiveness exercise into your prayer routines, force is
unlikely. If you can't forgive, if your pain is too vivid,
consider talking about your torment with a trusted, qualified therapist or spiritual counselor. Remember: you
don't have to rub elbows or be in fellowship with those
you forgive. Just *let go of your own agony.* If your abuser
is still crazed, abrasive, or unstable, then stay away. Also,
keep in mind that forgetting a hurtful episode could take
a while. However, forgetting is not your chief objective. It
is forgiveness that lets go of the pain, fury, and resent-
ments. Rage that you cannot or will not release lives on—
in *you.* Its energy contaminates *your* harmony, *your* interior comfort.

As soon as a resentful thought against anyone comes
up, we can educate ourselves to drop that thought. We can
visualize it leaving us, watch it float up to the sky, bursting
like a soap bubble, into so much nothingness. Or, simpler
still, we can choose to release erroneous thinking.

Here are some ideas for practicing forgiveness when
praying in the Spirit. *After* each session, be it five minutes
or sixty, when your emotions are settled and you are at
peace and your breathing has become fine and soft:

• Call to mind the name or face of anyone who has
  harmed or offended you and simply offer up that person—in prayer—to God. If that feels uncomfortable,

if you feel ill at ease, consider discussing your discomfort with a trusted counselor. And why not acknowledge that, in and of yourself, you are incapable of forgiving? Why not ask God to help you? This "casting of the burden" can accomplish seeming miracles.

- Call to mind the names or faces of those who have harmed or offended you and wish them all well with the words from 3 John 2: "Beloved, I wish above all things that thou mayest prosper and be in health, even as thy soul prospereth."

- Call to mind your *own* face when you've hurt, offended, or slighted anyone else, and especially if you feel bitter and resentful against someone. Forgive yourself, using the words from 3 John 2 or any preferred verse, and keep in mind that it is sometimes harder to forgive ourselves for the mistreatment we inflict (or ignore) than it is to forgive others.

- We must also forgive ourselves if we hang around with people who routinely abuse or devalue us. This is a tough habit to break, particularly when those hurtful individuals are family members. It may help to reflect on the counsel of psychiatrist Thomas Szasz: People "often treat others worse than they treat themselves, but they rarely treat anyone better. It is the height of folly to expect consideration and decency from a person who mistreats himself."[18]

In a CNN interview, Rabbi David Aaron shared one of his most beautiful childhood memories. His mother would sit beside him while reading *Winnie-the-Pooh* aloud, "and what was so special about that . . . [was] just lying there listening to Winnie-the-Pooh, because my mother was concentrating her entire presence. She was totally there for me. And that presence is the greatest gift we can ever receive."[19]

Rabbi Aaron added that according to the Kabbalah the greatest presence is "what we might call *God's* presence." That's exactly what we experience when we pray in the Spirit.

That's the daily drill and our contemplative practice. We bring our mind back to what's happening now. Simple observation lets us stop judging. It cultivates patience. That practice brings us into our sacred, right relationship with God's Presence. If we feel upset, fearful, disturbed, even inordinately excited, we can ask ourselves, "What thought, mood, or undercurrent of thought is separating me from the present moment?" Our answer ususally unites us with whatever's going on now.

Meister Eckhart, the great Christian mystic, keenly understood the nature of that oneness when he recalled Isaiah's word: we hold within ourselves "all truth in an essential manner."[20] That is our contemplative aim, for

What God gives is his being, and his being is his goodness, and his goodness is his love.

And I say further: to know this love in its empty [primal] purity is the reason for which we are born, the state of being we can never get enough of and the Kingdom without end.[21]

Throughout these pages I have suggested that for some activities and to some people and to some distressing states of mind, our spiritual truth asks us to say, "No more—enough is enough." Initially we do this with a personal stake in mind. We seek less stress. We crave more comfort. We'd like greater effectiveness in our world of affairs, and enhanced relationships.

Over time our own growth reveals the hidden truth: our very soul thirst for "the good wine." Then methods, contemplative or otherwise, only display the purpose of our life, the "state of being we can never get enough of—the Kingdom without end." So starts the fire, the divine intoxication.

Further Reading: Annotated Book List

Besides the many books already cited in the notes, a handful may be of special interest to those who want to study different facets of contemplative life, casual or otherwise. I've listed only *some* of my old favorites.

On Contemplative Prayer

Abhishiktānanda. *Prayer.* Delhi: ISPCK (P.O. Box 1583, Kashmere Gate, Delhi, India 110006), 1993.

This booklet is so pure, so rich with the voice of the Spirit—not at all academic or cerebral—and so thin a volume that I've misfiled it several times. I love this work and reread it frequently, especially after losing it for a while, reading it from back to front, from middle to outer ends. Whatever. The author was a French monk who lived in India for about thirty years as an adult. He found his Christian experience greatly enriched by the Hindu-Buddhist religious tradition.

Abbott Thomas Keating, O.C.S.O., M. Basil Pennington, O.C.S.O., and Thomas E. Clarke, S.J. *Finding Grace at the Center.* Still River, Mass.: St. Bede Publications, 1979.

Anyone interested in learning more about "centering prayer" might profit from reading this book. It's short, easy to read, and pretty traditional. Personally, I never could quite slog through the classic fourteenth-century book, *A Cloud of Unknowing,* which describes the earliest centering prayer.

Thomas Merton. *Contemplative Prayer.* New York: Image Books/Doubleday, 1969.

An easy, nontheoretical, inspiringly practical overview of contemplative prayer. One of the best overviews I've found. Includes short excerpts from different monastic traditions: Celtic, Syrian, Cistercian. Merton had a universal mind, hospitable to the principles of both Eastern meditation practices and more traditional Western approaches. His integrative love is obvious in these chapters.

Augustine Ichiro Okumura, O.C.D. *Awakening to Prayer.* Translated by Theresa Kazue Hiraki and Albert Masaru Yamato. Washington, D.C.: ICS Publications, 1994.

A bit more technical than Abhishiktānanda and Merton. In this case the author was born to a Buddhist family and later became a Carmelite priest. For him prayer is an intimate conversation. It requires the strictness of form and courtesy— total attention, the politeness of interior listening—*plus* the looseness of an ever-responsive flexibility, attentive to the Presence within. A rather traditional Christian discussion of prayer, the text nevertheless clearly reflects the author's Eastern influence. This uncomplicated, uncompromising discussion of prayer reveals a somewhat tough and rigorous "edge." I read this when in one of my slugfest spells.

Books with a Nonmonastic, Contemplative Feel

Oswald Chambers. *My Utmost for His Highest.* Urichville, Ohio: Discovery House Publisher/Barbour and Co., 1935.

A Christian devotional designed for daily reading as meditation and application. Incrementally, this study can build strength of worship and authentic faith. If you're mealy-mouthed about expressing your values or walking your spiritual talk, Chambers can straighten you out. He's a no-nonsense, "get real" practitioner. For me, meditating with Chambers for a year, every morning, was like attending boot camp. When the year was up, I started over again at the beginning and felt, "Thanks, I needed that."

Ram Dass, with Stephen Levine. *Grist for the Mill.* Santa Cruz, Calif.: Unity Press, 1976.

An oldie but goodie. A straightforward read about the intricacies of spiritual growth. It's pleasurable if you don't mind a decidedly New Age, seventies flavor. Ram Dass has a colloquial voice, informal, pop-culture yet profound. He tells stories about, say, Ramana Maharishi that amuse and instruct but his ideas could irritate mainstream readers.

Richard J. Foster. *Celebration of Discipline.* San Francisco: Harper San Francisco, 1978.

For those just starting to put their spiritual house in order,

Foster's guide to what he calls "inner," "outer," and "corporate" disciplines may prove invaluable. Orderly, a tad linear, Foster is nevertheless extremely thorough, and to me he's motivating.

Dorothy Gilman. *A New Kind of Country*. New York: Fawcett-Crest, 1978.

Gilman's book is only indirectly about contemplation and not really about praying in the Spirit. However, it absolutely relates. In this nonfiction work, the author of the Mrs. Pollifax series describes her "real-life odyssey of self-discovery," the solitary period she spent in Nova Scotia after raising two sons. Before that she had lived with parents, roommates, then a husband. Never alone. In her Nova Scotia experience no demands were made on her. Living alone, she writes, "I could, if I wanted, stay up all night and sleep all day, learn Russian, take a lover, play the phonograph at ear-bending volume, or be anything I wanted to be. . . . It was this that was foreign, not my surroundings. And it was frightening." Try it. You'll like it. Excellent for beginners in the solitary life. And not for women only.

Three Luminous Works that May Set Your Mind to Contemplating *While* You Read

Peter Browning, ed. *John Muir: In His Own Words*. Lafayette, Calif.: Great West Books, 1988.

I've cited Browning's book of Muir quotes in almost every book I've written. When I'm down, Muir cheers me up. When frazzled, Muir calms. I've packed *John Muir* in my suitcase for long business trips and feeling homesick. If you're a born contemplative, after reading Muir, you may end up donating your farm to a conservancy group, moving to a hut in the Rockies, or joining the Trappists or the Saint Clares. A saintly book. Buy it today. Give it as a Christmas gift to the members of your local city planning board if they even consider paving over one more inch of wilderness.

e. e. cummings. *100 Selected Poems*. New York: Grove Press, 1926.

If your spirit isn't quickened, your heart stirred up or even broken, by some line in this choice volume, please get help.

Walker Percy. *The Moviegoer*. New York: Ivy Books, 1960, 1961.

What can I say about Percy? Like Muir and e. e. cummings, he's a saint of sorts. He's God's man. A writer who calls us to awareness in the tradition of philosopher Søren Kierkegaard by describing the malaise or "sickness unto death" that engulfs us if we are not, as he puts it, "onto something" holy. *The Moviegoer* proves that Percy saw the holy in the dustiest, cobwebbiest corner. God bless you, W.P., e.e., and John Muir; you have blessed me.

Meditation and Contemplative Practice in Daily Life

Anne Bancroft. *Zen*. (Direct pointing to reality.) New York: Thames and Hudson, 1979.

The title says it all. One of the few books on Zen practice

with a decidedly mystical feel. An unassuming, easy-to-read, and beautifully illustrated book. For those who want to learn more about Zen "sitting."

Herbert Benson, M.D. *The Relaxation Response.* New York: Morrow, 1975.

Benson provides a Westernized version of classical meditation practice right in the book. By the time you're done, you might well have a makeshift, do-it-yourself meditation program. This book may have been updated recently, but I haven't read the new edition and don't know if it explains the original technique.

Harold Bloomfield, M.D. *Happiness: The TM Program: Psychiatry and Enlightenment.* New York: Dawn Press, 1976.

This book is out of print. Track it down if you can. It's the best, most convincing book I've read about the beneficial relationship that meditation has to stress management. Bloomfield, a psychiatrist and prolific author, is primarily writing about TM and does so in a lively, influential fashion.

Rufus M. Jones. *The Faith and Practice of the Quakers.* London: Methuen and Co.; Philadelphia: Religious Society of Friends, 1958.

A classic, inspirational overview of the spiritual "democracy" and praying in stillness that characterize Quaker meetings of worship. One could read this yearly and get something new out of it each time. Jones has a message of whopping potential value to clerics of every denomination who wonder why their flocks are leaving in droves. Let's face it, kids—people ache for a profound experience of the Divine.

John Cantwell Kiley, Ph.D. *Self-Rescue.* New York: Fawcett-Crest, 1977; Howell House, LA, Contemporary Books, Chic, 1990, 1992.

Self-Rescue tells us how to control, or manage, the "enemies" of our peace and offers what I'd call a walking meditation—a way to stay alert to the thoughts and feelings that disrupt our equilibrium. In the introduction to the original volume, William F. Buckley wrote, "Cleave to the practical wisdom of this book. It has found the contemporary idiom for an older consolation, 'The Lord is my shepherd. I shall not want.'"

Roy Masters. *How Your Mind Can Keep You Well.* Greenwich, Conn.: Fawcett-Crest, 1971, 1973.

Masters provides a specific meditation technique and some tough-love talk about spiritual regeneration and its demands.

Thomas Merton. *Contemplation in a World of Action.* New York: Image Books, 1973.

I carried this book with me on planes and read it nonstop when trying to figure out why I was gearing up for a contemplative life. For anyone who's immersed in business but who pines for a new depth of silent prayer, this is a book to cherish. For me, chapter 2 of the second part—on "The Cell"—is worth rereading every year.

Claudio Naranjo and Robert E. Ornstein. *On the Psychology of Meditation.* New York: Penguin, 1976.

Everything most people ever want to know about meditation is divulged here: its Eastern roots and Western application; why meditation extends our effectiveness; little secrets about various mantra sounds; what unites all true meditation despite differences in form. My favorite overview of the topic.

Ira Progoff. *At a Journal Workshop.* New York: Dialogue House Library, 1975.

A guide for using the author's seminar process. I believe Progoff, a professor and psychotherapist, studied with C. G. Jung in the mid–1890s. His journal method is a classic. This is the only journal book I've ever read that pulls my mind into a contemplative mode of thought rather than merely offering an intellectual or a touchy-feely, "How I felt at camp last summer" approach.

Brother Paul Quenon, Brother Guerric Plante, and Father Timothy Kelly. *Holy Folly: Short and Tall Tales from the Abbey of Gethsemani.* Windsor, Ontario: Black Moss Press (2450 Byng Rd., Windsor, Ontario, N8W3E8), 1998.

Charming, often droll, accounts of monks living and working at the Abbey of Gethsemani. The authors have brought the monastic tradition into the twenty-first century, where it belongs.

Marsha Sinetar. *Ordinary People as Monks and Mystics.* Mahwah, N.J.: Paulist Press, 1986.

It's said authors really write for themselves. When I'm wondering what on earth I'm doing with my life, I reread this book. Lots of down-to-earth case illustrations about ordinary people in various stages of setting up a reflective life as dictated by their aesthetic sensibilities and conscience.

Managing Time and Other Things

Robert Grundin. *Time and the Art of Living*. New York: Harper & Row, 1982.

If you're a slave to your obligations, a prisoner of your own projects or schedule, read this. A wonderful hodgepodge of thoughts on the politics of time and memory and great advice on how to cultivate an ear for the delicate music of our own sweet time.

Alan Lakein. *How to Get Control of Your Time and Your Life*. New York: Signet Books, 1973.

This is my preferred book on time management. I've used Lakein's method for years, for both personal and professional objectives. I've surveyed lots of other books on the topic, but I stick with this. Lakein is moderate. He's informal, neither overorganized nor too general. He gives us specifics for creating quiet time, dealing with information overload, and one gift-question, "What is the best use of my time, right now?"

Notes

Foreword

1. Paul Tillich, *The Courage to Be* (New Haven, London: Yale University Press, 1952), pp. 28–29.
2. *The Philokalia*, Vol. 1 (Boston, London: Faber and Faber, 1979), p. 11.
3. Ibid., p. 123.
4. *Meister Eckhart: Essential Sermons, Commentaries, Treatises and Defense* (Mahwah, N.J.: Paulist Press, 1981), p. 187.
5. Mahatma Gandhi, *All Men Are Brothers* (N.Y.: Continuum Publishing Corp., 1980), p. 162.
6. Marsha Sinetar, *Spiritual Intelligence* (Maryknoll, N.Y.: Orbis Books, 2000).

Introduction: First Words

1. Marsha Sinetar, *Living Happily Ever After* (New York: Random House, 1990).
2. Abhishiktānanda, *Prayer* (Delhi: ISPCK, 1993), p. 2.
3. Marsha Sinetar, *Holy Work* (New York: Crossroad Books,

1998) and *Mentor's Spirit* (New York: St. Martin's Press, 1998).

4. W. E. Vine, *An Expository Dictionary of New Testament Words*, 3rd ed. (Nashville: Thomas Nelson, n.d.), p. 490.

5. Father J. Borst, M.H.M., *A Method of Contemplative Prayer* (Bombay: Asian Trading Corp., 1973), p. 6.

Chapter 1: Shouldering the Beams of Love

1. Sister Benedicta Ward, S.L.G., *Wisdom of the Desert Fathers* (Oxford: SLG Press, 1975), p. 22.

2. Amanda Cross, *An Imperfect Spy* (New York: Ballantine Books, 1995), p. 139.

3. Jill Haak Adels, *The Wisdom of the Saints* (Oxford: Oxford University Press, 1987), p. 199.

4. Thomas Merton, *Contemplation in a World of Action* (New York: Image Books, 1973), p. 266.

5. Oswald Chambers, *My Utmost for His Highest* (Ohio: Barbour & Co., 1963), p. 327.

6. Abhishiktānanda, *Prayer* (Delhi: ISPCK, 1993), p. 21.

7. *U.S. News & World Report* (December 11, 1996): 88.

8. Yvonne Zipp, "Baby Boomers Driving the Spirituality Movement," *Christian Science Monitor*, December 15, 1998.

9. Thomas Merton, *Contemplative Prayer* (New York: Image Books/Doubleday, 1990), p. 9 (from the Foreword by Douglas Steere).

10. Marsha Sinetar, *Ordinary People as Monks and Mystics* (Mahwah, N.J.: Paulist Press, 1986).

11. Ibid., p. 5.

12. Thomas Merton, *Contemplation in a World of Action,* p. 352.

13. Brother Paul Quenon, Brother Guerric Plante, and Father Timothy Kelly, *Holy Folly* (Windsor, Ont.: Black Moss Press, 1998), p. 15.

14. Claudio Naranjo and Robert E. Ornstein, *On the Psychology of Meditation* (New York: Penguin Books/Esalen, 1977), p. 8 (emphasis in the original).

15. Abhishiktānanda, *Prayer,* p. 73.

16. From a booklet titled *Nonresistance* (Unity, Mo.: Unity School, n.d.), a condensation of a chapter from Amelda Octavia Shanklin, *What Are You?* (available from Unity School).

17. Ibid.

18. B. McGinn, *Meister Eckhart,* translated by E. Colledge, O.S.A. (Mahwah, N.J.: Paulist Press, 1981), p. 276.

19. Father J. Borst, MHM, *A Method of Contemplative Prayer* (Bombay: Asian Trading Corp. 1973), p. 6.

20. In *Positive Addiction* (New York: Harper & Row, 1976), William Glasser, M.D., discusses the framework and logic of helpful disciplines.

Chapter 2: The Hearing Ear, the Seeing Eye

1. *John Muir, In His Own Words,* edited by Peter Browning (Lafayette, Calif.: Great West Books, 1998), p. 31.

2. G.K. Chesterton, *Orthodoxy,* p. 112.

3. Jean Leclercq, *Bernard of Clairvaux and the Cistercian Spirit* (Kalamazoo, Mich.: Cistercian Publications, 1976).

4. Anonymous, *A Spiritual Friendship* (New York: Crossroad Publishing, 1999), p. 89.

5. Ibid., p. 87.

6. Ibid.

7. Quoted in Leslie R. Smith, *Four Keys to Prayer* (St. Louis: Bethany Press, 1962), p. 46.

Chapter 3: A Distinctive Reflection of Oneness

1. Dietrich Bonhoeffer, *The Cost of Discipleship* (New York: Macmillan, 1963).

2. Mahatma Gandhi, *All Men Are Brothers* (New York: Continuum Books, 1980), pp. 105–6.

3. Marsha Sinetar, *Holy Work* (New York: Crossroad Books, 1998).

4. Marsha Sinetar, *Spiritual Intelligence* (Maryknoll, N.Y.: Orbis Books, 2000).

5. Robert Kennedy, *Zen Spirit, Christian Spirit* (New York: Continuum, 1996), p. 58.

6. Ibid., p. 59.

7. *The Quimby Manuscripts,* edited by Horatio W. Dresser (New York: Thomas Y. Crowell, 1976), pp. 28–29.

8. Lewis Carroll, *Alice's Adventures in Wonderland* and *Through the Looking-Glass* (New York: New American Library/Signet Classic, 1960), p. 104.

9. Kathryn Kuhlman, *I Believe in Miracles* (Old Tappan, N.J.: Fleming H. Revell Co., 1979), p.14.

10. Marsha Sinetar, *Living Happily Ever After* (New York: Random House, 1990).

11. Rev. Marge Flotron, *The Teachings of Emma Curtis Hopkins* (audiotape) (Chicago: MTI). See also Emma Curtis Hopkins, *High Mysticism* (Marina del Rey, Calif.: De Vorss & Co., n.d.).

12. G. K. Chesterton, *St. Thomas Aquinas, The Dumb Ox* (New York: Image Books/Doubleday, 1956).

13. Ibid., p. 31.

14. Barbara Wilson, *Blue Windows* (New York: Picador USA, 1997), p. 82.

15. Augustine Ichiro Okumura, O.C.D., *Awakening to Prayer* (Washington, D.C.: ICO Publications, 1994), p. 50 (emphasis in the original).

16. Thomas Merton, *Contemplative Prayer* (New York: Image Books/Doubleday, 1990), p. 75.

17. Michael Murphy, *Golf in the Inner Kingdom* (New York: Dell, 1972), p. 128.

18. Harvey Penick and Bud Shrake, *Harvey Penick's Little Red Book* (New York: Simon & Schuster, 1992), p. 161.

19. Julian of Norwich, *Revelations of Divine Love* (London: Penguin Classic Books, 1996), p. 206.

20. Max Picard, *The World of Silence* (Southbend, Ind.: Regenery-Gateway, Inc., 1952).

21. Anonymous, *A Spiritual Friendship*. For the original of this Saint Francis anecdote, see *Saint Francis of Assisi: Writings and Early Biographies,* edited by Marion A. Habig (Chicago: Franciscan Herald Press, n.d.), pp. 731–32.

22. G. K. Chesterton, *Orthodoxy,* p. 55.

23. Thomas Merton, *Contemplative Prayer,* p. 94.

24. Dallas Willard, *The Spirit of the Disciplines* (San Francisco: Harper San Francisco, 1988).

25. *John Muir: In His Own Words,* edited by Peter Browning (Lafayette, Calif.: Great West Books, 1988), p. 25.

26. Baltasar Gracián, *The Art of Worldly Wisdom,* edited by C. Maurer (New York: Currency/Doubleday, 1992), p. 102.

Chapter 4: A Holy Untangling

1. Elsewhere and often (see, for example, *Holy Work,* New York: Crossroad Books, 1998), I've described *vocation* as the way we come into our own as individuals, within the context of our life with others. In hindsight we may realize that we've attended to our career, family, and spiritual life quite admirably. Augustine Ichiro Okumura, O.C.D. *Awakening to Prayer* (Washington, D.C.: ICO Publications, 1994), p. 52.

2. Augustine Ichiro Okumura, *Awakening to Prayer,* p. 52. Abhishiktānanda, *Prayer* (Delhi: ISPCK, 1993), p. 32.

3. Abhishiktānanda, *Prayer* (Mahwah, N.J.: Paulist Press, 1986), p. 32.

4. Marsha Sinetar, *Ordinary People as Monks and Mystics,* p. 23.

5. Max Picard, *The World of Silence* (Southbend, Ind.: Regenery-Gateway, Inc., 1952), p. 67.

6. Henry P. Van Dusen, *Dag Hammarskjöld* (New York: Harper & Row, 1967), p. x.

7. Ibid., p. 6.

8. Ibid., p. x.

9. Ibid., p. xi.

10. "A Perspective on Holidays: Billy Graham Interview," *Larry King Live,* December 25, 1998, CNN, Federal Document Clearing House transcript, p. 12.

Chapter 5: Learning to Walk Surely

1. Augustine Ichiro Okumura, O.C.D. *Awakening to Prayer* (Washington, D.C.: ICO Publications, 1994), p. 37.

2. Ibid., p. 27.

3. Ibid.

4. Raimon Panikkar, *A Dwelling Place for Wisdom* (Louisville: Westminster/John Knox Press, 1993), back cover.

5. Ibid., p. 156.

6. Ibid., p. 155.

7. Abbott Thomas Keating, O.C.S.O., M. Basil Pennington, O.C.S.O., and Thomas E. Clarke, S.J., *Finding Grace at the Center* (Still River, Mass.: St. Bede Publications, 1979), pp. 51–52.

8. G. K. Chesterton, *Orthodoxy*, p. 17.

9. "The Flower," in *George Herbert: The Country Parson, The Temple: Classics of Western Spirituality* (Mahwah, N.J.: Paulist Press, 1981), p. 292.

Chapter 6: Life as Wholesome Prayer

1. Leslie R. Smith, *Four Keys to Prayer* (St. Louis, Mo.: Bethany Press, 1962), p. 30.

2. Ram Dass, in collaboration with Stephen Levine, *Grist for the Mill* (Santa Cruz, Calif.: Unity Press, 1977), p. 45.

3. Augustine Ichiro Okumura, O.C.D. *Awakening to Prayer* (Washington, D.C.: ICO Publications, 1994), pp. 47, 27–28 (emphasis in the original).

4. Raymond E. F. Larsson, *Saints at Prayer* (New York: Coward-McCann, 1942).

5. Beth Bosk, "Plant Spirits—Part 2," *New Settler Interview* 116 (February–mid-March 1999): 6.

6. Ibid.

7. Saint Augustine, *The Confessions* (New York: Collier Macmillan, 1961), p. 107.

8. Marsha Sinetar, *Holy Work* (New York: Crossroad Books, 1998), see Part I.

9. G. K. Chesterton, *Saint Thomas Aquinas, The Dumb Ox* (New York: Image Books-Doubleday, 1956), pp. 100–102.

10. Ibid., p. 102.

11. Raimon Panikkar, *A Dwelling Place for Wisdom* (Louisville: Westminster/John Knox Press, 1993), p. 85.

12. Ibid.

13. Dietrich Bonhoeffer, *Life Together* (New York: Harper & Row, 1954), p. 33.

14. Ibid.

15. Thomas Merton, *Contemplation in a World of Action* (New York: Image Books, 1973), p. 366.

16. Thomas Merton, *Contemplative Prayer* (New York: Image Books/Doubleday, 1990), p. 94.

Chapter 7: An Infinite Progression

1. Walker Percy, *The Moviegoer* (New York: Ivy Books/Ballantine Books, 1961), p. 35.

2. *Merton by Those Who Knew Him Best,* edited by Paul Wilkes (New York: Harper & Row, 1984), p. 13.

3. Thomas Merton, *Contemplative Prayer* (New York: Image Books/Doubleday, 1990), p. 51–52 (emphasis in the original).

4. Ibid.

5. Ibid., p. 66.

6. John Briggs, *Fire in the Crucible* (Los Angeles: Jeremy P. Tarcher, 1990), p. 17.

7. Ibid., p. 18.

8. Marsha Sinetar, *Spiritual Intelligence* (Maryknoll, N.Y.: Orbis Books, 2000).

9. Marshall Stewart Ball, *Kiss of God: The Wisdom of a Silent Child* (Deerfield Beach, Fla.: Health Communications, 1999).

10. Karl Rahner, *Encounters with Silence* (Westminster, Md.: Christian Classics/Newman Press, 1960), p. 29.

11. Thomas Merton, *Contemplative Prayer,* p. 66.

12. Natalie Shainess, M.D., *Sweet Suffering* (New York: Wallaby Books/Simon & Schuster, 1984), p. 246.

13. Ibid.

14. Bicknell Young, "Establishing Day," in collection no. 2 (Santa Clara, Calif.: The Bookmark), p. 19.

15. Richard J. Foster, *Celebration of Discipline* (San Francisco: Harper San Francisco, 1978), pp. 58–60.

16. Ibid.

17. Jill Haak Adels, *The Wisdom of Saints* (New York: Oxford University Press, 1987), p. 142.

18. Thomas Szasz, *The Second Sin* (New York: Anchor Books, 1974), p. 53.

19. "Prescriptions for Spiritual Health" (interview), *Larry King Live*, March 16, 1999, Federal Documents Clearing House Transcript, p. 12.

20. Meister Eckhart, *The Essential Sermons, Commentaries, Treatises, and Defense,* translated by E. Colledge and B. McGinn (New York: Paulist Press, 1961), p. 184.

21. Ibid., p. 195.